A Multidisciplinary Approach to Embodiment

This is a collection of pithy and accessible essays on the nature and implications of human embodiment, that explore the concept of "human being" in the most unprecedented manner through seemingly disparate academic disciplines.

With contributions from key researchers from around the world, this book takes up embodiment through the lens of "new materialism." It eschews the view that human beings are debased by materiality and creates a vision of humans as fully embodied creatures situated in a richly populated living planet. The essays in this volume will illustrate and foster new materialist thought in areas including psychology, astrophysics, geology, biology, sociology, philosophy, and the performing arts. The book's engaging and enlightening content is made accessible to readers with relatively little background in the various academic disciplines.

This is an important and fascinating text which invites readers to explore and expand their understanding and experience of embodiment. It will be particularly useful for postgraduate students and scholars of theoretical and philosophical psychology, philosophy of the mind, and social and cultural anthropology.

Nancy K. Dess, PhD, is Professor of Psychology at Occidental College, USA, with primary expertise in experimental and comparative psychology. Beyond her empirical research, she advocates for multilevel integrative approaches to complex phenomena, the democratizing potential of science, and fully embodied conceptualizations of the lives of humans and other animals.

Advances in Theoretical and Philosophical Psychology

Series Editor: Brent D. Slife, Brigham Young University

https://www.routledge.com/psychology/series/TPP

"Embodiment is a topic that has greatly influenced the recent multidisciplinary study of human minds. Nancy Dess's new edited book offers a vivid, fresh look at the ways embodiment unfolds within many forms of human action and meaning-making. Embodiment is not just the brain or the biological body, but a dynamic organization that includes brains and bodies interacting with the cultural, historical world in the service of adaptive action. These essays are all a delight to read and offer many new insights into the ways embodiment defines who we are as unique human beings in shared worlds of embodied inter-subjectivity."
—*Raymond W. Gibbs, Jr., former Distinguished Professor of Psychology, University of California, Santa Cruz, USA*

"A decade ago, I thought I was being radically inclusive when I wrote an essay entitled, 'Embodiment as a unifying perspective for psychology.' But this delightfully readable volume of short essays greatly expands the embodiment program by documenting contributions of embodiment to anthropology, biology, communication, education, gender studies, geology, kinesiology, performing arts, philosophy, physics, political science, psychology, and sociology. I recommend it to all who are interested in human being."
—*Arthur Glenberg, Director of the Laboratory for Embodied Cognition at Arizona State University, USA and member of INICO, Universidad de Salamanca, Spain*

"This collection of essays takes up the difficult challenge of approaching embodied existence from different perspectives while breaking away from the domination by the usual viewpoints. A very welcome opening up of the wealth of perspectives, with the unifying ambition to bring out the multifaceted character of the embodied human life."
—*Helena De Preester, Professor of Philosophy, University of Applied Sciences and Arts (Ghent) and Ghent University, Belgium*

"This dazzling volume takes multidisciplinarity to a new level. From cells to stars and from anxiety to avatars, leading researchers and emerging luminaries offer an expansive and inspiring exploration that will have much to teach anyone interested in embodiment."
—*Jesse Prinz, Distinguished Professor of Philosophy and Director of the Committee for Interdisciplinary Science Studies at the City University of New York, Graduate Center, USA*

"A Multidisciplinary Approach to Embodiment: Understanding Human Being stands out from the crowd. This highly original collection achieves true interdisciplinarity, bringing together contributions from the social sciences, humanities, and biomedical sciences to summarize current thinking on body, mind and world, from multiple perspectives."

—Daniel Casansanto, Associate Professor of Human Development and Psychology and Director of the Experience and Cognition Laboratory at Cornell University, USA

A Multidisciplinary Approach to Embodiment

Understanding Human Being

Edited by Nancy K. Dess

R Routledge

Taylor & Francis Group

NEW YORK AND LONDON

First published 2021
by Routledge
52 Vanderbilt Avenue, New York, NY 10017

and by Routledge
2 Park Square, Milton Park, Abingdon, Oxon, OX14 4RN

Routledge is an imprint of the Taylor & Francis Group, an informa business

© 2021 Taylor & Francis

Library of Congress Cataloging-in-Publication Data
Names: Dess, Nancy Kimberly, editor.
Title: A multidisciplinary approach to embodiment:
understanding human being / edited by Nancy K. Dess.
Identifiers: LCCN 2020019082 (print) | LCCN 2020019083 (ebook) |
ISBN 9780367370275 (hardback) | ISBN 9780429352379 (ebook)
Subjects: LCSH: Mind and body. | Social psychology. | Ethnology.
Classification: LCC BF161 .M865 2020 (print) |
LCC BF161 (ebook) | DDC 128—dc23
LC record available at https://lccn.loc.gov/2020019082
LC ebook record available at https://lccn.loc.gov/2020019083

ISBN: 978-0-367-37027-5 (hbk)
ISBN: 978-0-367-56047-8 (pbk)
ISBN: 978-0-429-35237-9 (ebk)

DOI: 10.4324/9780429352379

Typeset in Times New Roman
by codeMantra

Contents

Contributors

Bibi Bakare-Yusuf, PhD, is co-founder and publishing director of one of Africa's leading publishing houses, Cassava Republic Press and co-founder of Tapestry Consulting, a boutique research and training company focused on gender, sexuality, and transformational issues in Nigeria.

Louise Barrett, PhD, is Canada Research Chair (Tier I) in Cognition, Evolution and Behaviour at the University of Lethbridge, Alberta, Canada.

Marcia Bjornerud, PhD, is Professor of Geosciences at Lawrence University in Appleton, Wisconsin, USA.

Gregory A. Bryant, PhD, is Professor of Communication and Member of the Center for Behavior, Evolution, and Culture at the University of California at Los Angeles, California, USA.

Anthony Chemero, PhD, is Professor of Philosophy and Psychology at the University of Cincinnati, Cincinnati, Ohio, USA.

Gaetan Chevalier, PhD, is Senior Research Scientist of the Laboratory for Mind-Body Signaling and Energy Research in the Department of Developmental & Cell Biology and the Susan Samueli Integrative Health Institute at the University of California, Irvine, California, USA.

Giovanna Colombetti, PhD, is Associate Professor of Philosophy in the Department of Sociology, Philosophy, and Anthropology at the University of Exeter, UK.

Nancy K. Dess, PhD, is Professor of Psychology at Occidental College in Los Angeles, California, USA.

Tiffany Field, PhD, is Professor in the Departments of Pediatrics, Psychology, and Psychiatry, and Director of the Touch Research

Institute at the University of Miami Miller School of Medicine, Miami, Florida, USA.

Samantha Frost, PhD, is Professor in the Department of Political Science, the Department of Gender and Women's Studies, and the Unit for Criticism and Interpretive Theory at the University of Illinois, Urbana-Champaign, Illinois, USA.

Susan Goldin-Meadow, PhD, is Beardsley Ruml Distinguished Service Professor in the Departments of Psychology and Comparative Human Development at the University of Chicago, Chicago, Illinois, USA.

Patricia Adair Gowaty, PhD, is Distinguished Professor Emerita in the Department of Ecology and Evolutionary Biology at the University of California at Los Angeles, USA, and Distinguished Research Professor Emerita in the Odum School of Ecology at the University of Georgia, Athens, Georgia, USA.

Barbara Helm, PhD, is Professor for Biological Rhythms of Natural Organisms in the Groningen Institute for Evolutionary Life Sciences (GELIFES) at the University of Groningen, The Netherlands, and Visiting Professor in the Institute of Biodiversity, Animal Health & Comparative Medicine, University of Glasgow, UK.

Fernanda Herrera, PhD, is a researcher in the Department of Communication at Stanford University, Palo Alto, California, USA.

Fred Keijzer, PhD, is Associate Professor in the Faculty of Philosophy of the University of Groningen, the Netherlands.

Shin Lin, PhD, is Professor and Founding Director of the Laboratory for Mind-Body Signaling and Energy Research in the Department of Developmental & Cell Biology and the Susan Samueli Integrative Health Institute at the University of California, Irvine, California, USA.

Anne Mangen, PhD, is Professor in the Norwegian Reading Centre at the University of Stavanger, Stavanger, Norway.

Maurizio Meloni, PhD, is ARC Future Fellow and Associate Professor at the Alfred Deakin Institute for Citizenship and Globalisation (ADI) at Deakin University, Australia.

Barbara Gail Montero, PhD, is Professor of Philosophy at the City University of New York, USA.

Aidan Moran, PhD, was/late Professor of Cognitive Psychology and Director of the Psychology Research Laboratory at University College Dublin, Ireland.

Arun Saldanha, PhD, is Professor in the Department of Geography, Environment and Society, University of Minnesota, USA.

Iris Schrijver, MD, a physician specialized in laboratory medicine and molecular genetics, Adjunct Professor of Pathology in the School of Medicine at Stanford University, California, USA. She also is Medical Director of Clackamas Volunteers in Medicine in Oregon City, Oregon, USA.

Karel Schrijver, PhD, is an astrophysicist and science writer whose work focuses on how the magnetic activity of stars shapes the environments of stars and the habitability of planets. He headed the investigations for two of NASA's most powerful instruments observing the Sun and led educational programs about star–planet connections for young researchers.

Sheldon Solomon, PhD, is Professor of Psychology at Skidmore College, Saratoga Springs, New York, USA.

Paula Thomson, PsyD, is Professor of Kinesiology at California State University, Northridge (US) and Professor Emerita/Senior Scholar at York University (Toronto, Ontario, Canada). She is also a licensed clinical psychologist in private practice in Los Angeles, California, USA.

John Toner, PhD, is Lecturer in Sports Coaching and Performance at the University of Hull, UK.

Luis P. Villarreal, PhD, is Professor Emeritus in the Department of Molecular Biology and Biochemistry at the University of California, Irvine, California, USA.

Guenther Witzany, PhD, is an independent philosopher at Telos – Philosophische Praxis, in Vogelsangstraße, Buermoos, Austria.

Foreword by Series Editor

Brent D. Slife

Psychologists need to face the facts. Their commitment to empiricism for answering disciplinary questions does not prevent pivotal questions from arising that cannot be evaluated exclusively through empirical methods, hence the title of this series: *Advances in Theoretical and Philosophical Psychology*. For instance, such moral questions as, "What is the nature of a good life?" are crucial to psychotherapists but are not answerable through empirical methods alone. And what of the methods themselves? Many have worried that our current psychological means of investigation are not adequate for fully understanding the person (e.g., Schiff, 2019). How do we address this concern through empirical methods without running headlong into the dilemma of methods investigating themselves? Such questions are in some sense philosophical, to be sure, but the discipline of psychology cannot advance even its own empirical agenda without addressing questions like these in defensible ways.

How then should the discipline of psychology deal with such distinctly theoretical questions? We could leave the answers exclusively to professional philosophers, but this option would mean that the conceptual foundations of the discipline, including the conceptual framework of empiricism itself, are left to scholars who are *outside* the discipline. As undoubtedly helpful as philosophers are and will be, this situation would mean that the people doing the actual psychological work, psychologists themselves, are divorced from the people who formulate and reformulate the conceptual foundations of that work. This division of labor would not seem to serve the long-term viability of the discipline.

Instead, the founders of psychology — thinkers such as Wundt, Freud, and James — recognized the importance of psychologists in formulating their own foundations. These parents of psychology not only did their own theorizing, in cooperation with many other disciplines, they also realized the significance of psychologists continuously *re*-examining these theories and philosophies. This re-examination process allowed for the people most directly involved in and knowledgeable about the discipline to be the ones to decide *whether* changes were needed, and *how* such changes would best be implemented. This book series is dedicated to that task, the examining and re-examining of psychology's foundations.

Book Foreword

The present book exemplifies this re-examination process beautifully. One of the long-neglected foundations of psychology is its dualism, in all its forms. Indeed, one of those forms is a prominent aspect of many books in this series, the duality of fact and value or objectivity and subjectivity. Here, a set of facts — the "objective" realm — is considered separable from values or subjectivity. This type of dualism is perhaps most easily seen in many conceptions of science (or perhaps scientism, Gantt & Williams, 2019). The subjectivity of researchers (values, assumptions) is thought to be separable from the objectivity of data. Most psychological researchers will readily admit that subjective and objective factors are *difficult* to separate, but they presume through many modern methods that such factors *should* be separated (Gantt & Williams, 2019).

The fascinating thing about the present book is that it challenges an entirely different type of dualism, the separability of mind and body. Now this dualism has long been viewed as a problem, especially in the neurosciences. However, few of those who have problematized mind–body dualism have actually offered viable solutions to the problem. Either the "solution" is what some have called a "one-sided dualism" (Hedges & Burchfield, 2005; Slife & Hopkins, 2005) where a variation on materialism is offered that contains hidden non-materialist factors and assumptions. Or the so-called solution does not lead to alternative psychological research and practices that are useful.

On these issues in particular, I invite the reader to consider the embodiment conception of the present book as a more viable solution to the problem of mind–body dualism (which can itself imply many other dualisms, such as nature-nurture). Embodiment is not only conceptually and philosophically rigorous but also pregnant with heuristic insights and practical ramifications. No conception is unassailable, of course, but even a modest scan of the book will reveal its intellectual rigor and pragmatic relevance. Its chapters are wonderfully diverse, with authors from widely divergent disciplines and nationalities. Yet what is nicely thematized across the book's many accessible chapters is a reclaiming (from Merleau-Ponty) of not only the mind as embodied but also perhaps a "mentalized" body with a kind of wisdom and rationality. Suddenly the brain is no longer the center of information processing, and the body is no longer merely inert meat.

So buckle your seatbelt, dear reader, because you are in for a wild ride of "ah-has" and "wows" — a grand combination of revolutionary perspective and practical implication that will doubtless establish this book as a profound resource for years to come.

References

Gantt, E., & Williams, R. (2018). *On hijacking science: Exploring the nature and consequences of overreach in psychology.* London: Routledge.

Hedges, D., & Burchfield, C. (2005). The assumptions and implications of the neurobiological approach to depression. In Slife, B., Reber, J., & Richardson, F. (Eds.), *Critical thinking about psychology: Hidden assumptions and plausible alternatives.* Washington, DC: APA Books.

Schiff, B. (2019). *Situating qualitative methods in psychological science.* London: Routledge.

Slife, B., & Hopkins, R. (2005). Alternative assumptions for neuroscience. In Slife, B., Reber, J., & Richardson, F. (Eds.), *Critical thinking about psychology: Hidden assumptions and plausible alternatives.* Washington, DC: APA Books.

Preface by Book Editor

Nancy K. Dess

It is dangerous to show man [*sic*, hereafter for he/his/him] too clearly how much he resembles the beast without at the same time showing him his greatness. It is also dangerous to allow him too clear a vision of his greatness without his baseness. It is even more dangerous to leave him in ignorance of both. But it is very profitable to show him both

(Blaise Pascal, Pensées, 1669)

In this passage, Pascal builds on René Descartes' distinction between the material body and the immaterial mind: The body debases humans by *connecting* them to the beast; the mind elevates humans by *separating* them from the beast. Yet Pascal warns against what can be termed *hegemonic human exceptionalism* – a dominant discourse that perpetuates fascination with the human mind and its presumed specialness. That exceptionalist spotlight banishes to darkness other animals and human creatureliness.

A Multidisciplinary Approach to Embodiment rejects Pascal's view that humans are debased by similarities to other animals or made great by differences from them, but it embraces his warning about ignorance of human creatureliness. Collectively, the essays articulate a vision of humans as fully embodied creatures on a richly populated planet derived from stardust. In so doing, they aim to transform how readers think and feel about being human, alive, and earthly.

Why heed advice from hundreds of years ago? Body troubles survived the 17th century. In *Denial of Death* (1973), anthropologist Ernest Becker described how humans everywhere cope with the body's troublingly temporary nature by denying mortality in creative ways. Two 20th-century intellectual movements can be read as death-denying or, at least, as side-stepping the deep implications of embodiment:

- A central trope in the *Cognitive Revolution* was the human mind as information processor. Whereas ancient Egyptian morticians preserved most of the body while discarding the brain, cognitive scientists revered the brain as the hardware for a computer-like mind and discarded the rest of the body as an inert input/output device.
- *Postmodernism* brought forward the idea that through human meaning making, the body comes into being as a symbol or position in decentralized webs of norms and power. Inquiry into human bodies in terms of other-than-discursive processes was irrelevant, if not prohibited on grounds that it "biologized" or "naturalized" humans.

For all these movements accomplished, neither unsettled veneration of the human mind. Other animals remained in shadow and the human body remained ethereal, more an avatar than a large, bipedal animal who, in addition to deciding, remembering, and making meaning, also breathes, bleeds, bellows, and births babies.

Today, Cartesian mind/body dualism still leaks out in phrases such as "mind/body relationship" and "mind over matter." Uttering "humans and animal" telegraphs that humans are not animals, and referring to persons as "animals" usually aims to insult and "de*hu*ma*ni*ze." These taken-for-granted meanings expose *the thinking human* as an implicit norm from which fully embodied animals deviate.

In academe, dualism lingers in the "nature/nurture" dichotomy and its kin ("biological/social," "innate/learned") despite consensus that they are profoundly flawed. They reinforce and are reinforced by scholarly fragmentation. *Human*ities carry on in departments, buildings, and conferences separate from sciences. "Social" sciences are separated from "natural" sciences as if sociality is not natural, and "life" sciences are separated from "physical" sciences as if living things are not physical. Moreover, scientific disciplines comprise a status hierarchy, with disciplines focused on the inanimate – the "hard sciences" – at the top and status declining as demographic diversity and concern with complex sociality rise. Scholarship transcending these sociostructural boundaries remains rare.

Change is afoot. Thinkers across the scholarly landscape are engaging embodiment in fresh ways. The new approaches depart from both reductionistic views of the body and human-centric mentalism. Bodies are being viewed as at once universal and varied, solid and permeable, stable and mutable, eternal and ephemeral. An overarching principle is that the living human body has been and continues to be shaped and deployed through recursive interactions within and between bodies, embedded in dynamic intersecting ecologies.

This emerging view infuses the following collection of essays by an international constellation of scholars in anthropology, biology, cognitive science, communication, education, gender studies, geology, kinesiology, performing arts, philosophy, physics, political science, psychology, and sociology. Humans receive more attention than other animals, but not as a distraction from debasement or annihilation. Here, the focus draws purposeful attention to one kind of animal – our kind – living among others, with myriad lenses aimed at levels of organization from subcellular to cosmic and on time scales from deep time to momentary.

The exploration herein begins with an *Introduction* that lays out the justification for an approach to embodiment of unprecedented scope. The ensuing essays are organized around five themes: *Being, Engaging, Coordinating, (Re)Locating,* and *Healing.* Each essay begins with a concise statement that orients readers to the thesis and concludes with a short list of resources **(For Sources and Further Reading)** containing source materials, technical details, and supporting evidence that supplement the text, along with more food for thought. The *Epilogue* conjures the future by tracing the trajectory from modern cognitivism through the emergence of *embodied cognition* enthusiasms to a conceptualization of *embodiment* that charts for the scholarly community a rich, integrative path forward.

This book invites readers to expand their understanding and experience of embodiment. It also reveals academic disciplines as seemingly disparate as psychology, physics, and performing arts to be interconnected via hubs and bridges, not contained within silos. By literally "fleshing out" humans for tomorrow's scholars, this book plants seeds for a transdisciplinary metatheory of *human being* – and for the nimble, diverse, just academy needed to fulfill its promise.

Introduction: Face It or Replace It?

Why Computational Metaphors Fall Short and Why We Need a New Approach

Louise Barrett

> We are living creatures, so comparisons to machines and com-
> putational devices will always fall short as metaphors for how we
> make sense of the worlds in which we live.

When Shakespeare wrote that Juliet was the sun, he didn't mean
she was a giant ball of flaming gas, or that she lived eight million
miles away from earth. He meant she was the center of Romeo's
world, the life-giving force without which he could not survive.
That's how it goes with metaphors. We don't apply them literally;
we use them to capture a certain quality of the object in question, a
way of seeing through one thing to gain a fresh appreciation of another. Similarly, in science, we use metaphors to help us think about
the things we don't understand in terms of the things we do. Without the metaphor, we would have no name to describe the abstract
concepts and complex processes we have to grapple with. Using a
metaphor turns the abstract into something concrete and provides
us with a guide to discovery.

   I raise this issue because we seem to have lost control of our metaphors when thinking about brains and cognition. Descriptions of
brains as computers, and neural activity and associated psychological processes as information processing, are now taken quite literally. For example, in an op-ed for the *New York Times*, published
a few years ago, Gary Marcus bluntly told us all to "face it, your
brain is a computer," strongly implying that using metaphors is not
a means to kick-start new ways of thinking, but a way to identify
the "right" way of thinking about things. For Marcus, Descartes'
idea of the brain as a hydraulic pump, for example, was just one
in a long list of failed metaphors that could never give us the right

answer. But Descartes was not wrong as such, he was simply using the best metaphor he had at his disposal to make familiar what was otherwise deeply unfamiliar and difficult to grasp. Obviously, times change, knowledge grows, we think differently, and we adopt new and better metaphors. Descartes was a man of his time, and if we have a better metaphor than he did, it's because we have gained more knowledge of the brain. Marcus goes further than this, however, suggesting that the computational brain is not simply a more useful metaphor than a hydraulic pump, but precisely the right comparison: Brains *are* computers, and those who object to this idea are, quite simply, wrong. All we have to do, he says, is figure out what *kind* of computers they are.

But here's the thing: The objections that Marcus raises and then dismisses against the computer metaphor – that computers are serial, stored-program machines whereas brains are parallel; that computers are digital and brains are analog; that computers cannot generate emotions like humans – is like assuming Shakespeare was, in fact, referring to Juliet's resemblance to a giant ball of gas. Such objections make his argument sound more plausible but fail to capture the metaphor's essence. The heart of the original computer metaphor is the idea that brains construct an internal model of our environment, and that this internal representation is what allows us to act efficiently and effectively. Like computers, brains take certain inputs, manipulate these in various ways to generate our perception of the world, and then compute a set of outputs that instruct our bodies how to act. This is the job of the brain, so the argument goes, because the inputs our senses receive are too impoverished to allow us to cope with the world around us. The flat, upside-down image on our retina, for example, has to be converted into our dynamic three-dimensional view of the world. Our contact with reality is therefore indirect, via the representational model our brain builds, and not with the world itself. This view, as it turns out, was more or less what Descartes suggested as well, so the gap between Descartes's and the computer metaphor is not so great as Marcus makes it seem.

The idea that brains are biological computers and that cognition is a process of computation is a legacy of the original artificial intelligence project of the 1950s. Its guiding assumption was that intelligence could be modeled by computers, and it focused on precisely the kinds of representation-heavy abilities, like language skills and mathematics, that were thought to epitomize intelligent behavior. This approach failed to deliver on its promise. As Marcus admits, we are no closer to understanding the brain in computational terms than we were 60 years ago. So perhaps we should change our metaphors, and so change the job description of the brain.

Instead of thinking of brains as representational, we can view them as "performative": Their job is not to model the world around us, but to guide and control the actions of our bodies in an inherently dynamic, unpredictable world. Rodney Brooks, the MIT roboticist, makes the argument this way: Four billion years of evolution were, in the main, spent refining the perception–action mechanisms that guide effective action in the world. It took an enormously long time to build insect-level intelligence, while those things we think of as highly intelligent human capacities – language, logic, mathematics, chess – evolved very rapidly in less than a blink of evolution's eye. These distinctively human, representation-heavy capacities must therefore have been pretty easy to implement once the former was in place, Brooks argues. This means we would do better trying to understand how whole animals cope with changeable environments, rather than assuming that investigating the computing power of brains in isolation will allow us to understand how flexible, adaptive behavior is produced.

Brooks was the pioneer of an alternative behavior-based robotics, which demonstrated convincingly that flexible, adaptive, intelligent behavior does not require a representation-heavy computational model to achieve. He built robots with bodies that could sense and act in ways that allowed the robot to "use the world as its own best model" and didn't worry about providing them with any kind of central processing unit or "brain." After all, why go to the expense of representing the world, when the world itself contains all the information needed? As inventor of the Roomba, the vacuum cleaner that uses precisely these principles to clean your house all by itself, the strength of Brooks' approach is clear: Ten million Roomba owners can't be wrong.

Rather than viewing the brain as the only factor responsible for adaptive behavior, this "embodied" view of cognition regards the brain as part of a dynamic system in which brains, bodies, and environment all come together to generate intelligent action. That is, cognitive processes are grounded in action, and are not purely brain-based phenomena, but also exploit both the body and environment so that problems can be solved more cheaply than via energetically expensive brain tissue. If you've ever wondered why a seahorse looks so boxy and square, for example, it is because a tail with a square cross-section enables firmer anchoring to marine plants than does a circular one, which reduces the need for fine motor control. The importance of bodies is also apparent among animals that are well endowed with brain tissue, such as New Caledonian crows. These birds have the ability to both make and use tools, but it is not apparent that their brains are any larger or more complex than those of the other members of the crow family. What New Caledonian crows do possess, however, are very straight bills and forward-facing eyes that improve their ability to grasp and visually guide the stick-like tools they use to acquire food, giving them the edge over other crow species.

Marcus, and other proponents of the standard cognitivist view, give the impression that the representational–computational brain is the only game in town. Although we humans can and do deal with representations (after all, by reading the words on this page, this is precisely what you are doing now), we need to entertain the possibility that this is a nifty trick that humans developed over the course of our own particular history, and not something that all brains everywhere have evolved to do. It may also be useful to continue using computational–representational models in certain areas of neuroscience and psychology, while recognizing that such models are, in all probability, wrong about the way brains actually work. Brains are not magical, as Marcus rightly says, but that doesn't mean they must obey the laws of computation. Work in artificial life, behavior-based robotics and embodied cognition suggests we are reaching the limits of the computer metaphor, and it may be time to try something new.

Perhaps another useful metaphor, as Daniel Nicholson suggests, is to think of organisms as more like candle flames than machines. A flame has an enduring and stable form, but this comes about as a result of a continually ongoing set of dynamic processes. This metaphor highlights a crucial difference: Machines can only take part in processes, but organisms *are* processes. You can turn a machine off, and it will still be there, but not so an organism (well, it will for a bit, but we call that being dead). In this alternative view, organisms are thus seen as leaky processes spreading out across brain, body, and world. Similarly, we may be able to advance our understanding of ourselves and other organisms – and hopefully improve all planetary life – by recognizing the need for a similarly leaky process of knowledge production, one that regards disciplinary boundaries as entirely porous and focuses on examining common areas of interest from a variety of intersecting perspectives. The essays in this book make for an excellent start.

For Sources and Further Reading

Barrett, L. (2015). Beyond the brain: How body and environment shape animal and human minds. Princeton, NJ: Princeton University Press.

Barrett, L. (2016). Why brains are not computers, why behaviorism is not satanism, and why dolphins are not aquatic apes. *The Behavior Analyst*, *39*(1), 9–23.

Brooks, R. (2002). *Robot: The future of flesh and machines*. London: Penguin Books.

Leary, D. E. (Ed.). (1994). *Metaphors in the history of psychology*. Cambridge, UK: Cambridge University Press.

Marcus, G. (2015). Face it, your brain is a computer. *New York Times*, June 27, 2015. https://www.nytimes.com/2015/06/28/opinion/sunday/face-it-your-brain-is-a-computer.html

Nicholson, D. J. (2018). Reconceptualizing the organism: From complex machine to flowing stream. In Nicholson, D. J., & Dupré, J. (Eds.), *Everything flows: Towards a processual philosophy of biology* (pp. 139–166). New York: Oxford University Press.

Part I

Being

Of what is a human body made? How does it appear when viewed through lenses of deep space, deep time, or a microscope? What makes a body alive, or dead? How big or complicated do bodies need to be for social life to emerge? How much of a human body is actually human? The essays in this section take up these questions at levels of organization from cosmic to subcellular and on time scales from geological to momentary.

1 The Matter of Life and Death

How Humans Embody the Universe

Iris Schrijver and Karel Schrijver

The human body and the network of terrestrial life that enables its existence are always in flux, creating and exchanging countless molecules, made mostly of elements forged inside stars or in the explosions that end their existence. Captured from interstellar space as the solar system took shape, these essential elements are shared by all life on Earth, shattering the notion of independent existence and highlighting universal interconnectedness.

The unfathomable vastness and the staggering hierarchy of scales in the Universe defy immediate experience, complete understanding, and even our imagination because astronomical numbers reach beyond any sense of practical reality. Yet, they fascinate. They spark scientific research as much as philosophical discussion and compel us to consider how human life fits in. An exploration of the myriad connections between life and the Universe leads to a startling, perhaps unsettling conclusion: We are nothing even as we encompass everything. But how, exactly, is that manifested?

All measurable time originated 14.6 billion years ago with the Big Bang that hurled the Universe into existence. The ensuing inferno of expanding and collapsing gaseous clouds eventually gave birth to uncounted galaxies, of which we can see only a trillion or two. In each of these, in cycle after cycle of successive generations, billions of planetary systems took shape around stars that sustain nuclear fusion until they fade away or explode. The Universe may seem ageless, but the countless individual objects contained in it, from entire galaxies to individual rocks, have materialized in ongoing processes of formation to obliteration. By current estimates, our own Milky Way Galaxy alone contains 100–400 billion stars and a multiple of that number in planets. Out of those, perhaps ten billion might have Earth-like characteristics, with some potentially harboring life. All are located lightyears beyond the Solar System and remain out of reach for humanity.

At 4.6 billion years old, the Solar System is the home of Earth and seven other planets. Earth is a mid-sized planet, currently support-ing about 7.7 billion people and the only place, anywhere, known to sustain life. Based on microfossils of the earliest single-celled organisms, life on Earth began at least 2.5 billion years ago, but ancillary evidence suggests that life emerged around 3.9 billion years ago. Quite possibly on a random Tuesday afternoon. Earth orbits a sole star, the Sun, which is a middleweight star projected to continue its nuclear fusion for another five billion years. Given its life-sustaining energy, that should come as a relief! Apart from the Sun and the planets, the Solar System includes other heavenly bodies such as comets, which are frozen time capsules made of gas, dust, and rock from interstellar space. Comets date back to the for-mation of the Solar System and are made from the same materials. Although usually unnoticed, comet matter continues to sprinkle onto Earth at a rate that is currently about 260,000 pounds per day.

As inhabitants of Earth, human beings have a body that mirrors the complexity of the Universe. With a ballpark figure of 50 trillion cells per average body, the cells in a single human body outnumber the stars in our Galaxy 500 to 1 and Earth's population around 10,000 to 1. Within each cell reside approximately the same as-tounding number of atoms, a fraction of which make spiraling clus-ters that contain our DNA, an extremely thin string some two yards long so tightly coiled up that, if unfolded, it could wrap around its cell thousands of times. Analogous to events elsewhere in the Universe, human existence is characterized by cycles of arising and passing – not only in the literal sense of birth and death but also in terms of what happens in the body during a lifetime. The tissues and their constituent cells that shape human bodies enable countless as-tonishingly coordinated functions. However, the stresses within the functioning body and those imposed from outside frequently cause cells to fail. In order to keep things running smoothly, entire cells and their building blocks are replaced and regenerated in a process that involves millions of cells every second, although this renewal becomes less efficient over time as evidenced by the aging process.

Hidden in the background of each lived life, the inner workings of the human body are always in motion, taking care of a continuously occurring vast number of adjustments. The hundreds of different cell types have life spans ranging from days to years but overall are replaced about every seven years. This cell turnover amounts to the weight of an entire human body each year! Cell contents turn over with an even greater frequency. Take water, for example, which makes up the largest bulk of body weight and volume and is completely exchanged in a matter of weeks, at most. Water is but one of an immense collective of molecules found in every cell that includes the four major classes of organic compounds: carbohydrates, proteins, lipids, and nucleic acids. These facilitate functionality, enable energy usage and storage, and balance all of life's chemical reactions. But the human body does not make all of these itself, and those that it does make require building blocks and energy to be put together. That energy is supplied by combining the oxygen we breathe with the food we eat, but not directly. Between ingestion and use sits digestion that is enabled by the microbiome: Human beings are colonized by hundreds of species of bacteria. These organisms, on surface areas outside and inside the body, exist with us in a symbiotic relationship. Astonishingly, they outnumber the human cells of the body. And whereas bacteria are most prominently known for their disease-causing capacity, the microbiome categorically deserves more positive press. Not only does it process our food at the molecular level, it affects mind-states such as mood and helps strengthen our immune defenses. Ultimately, it critically contributes to the maintenance of health.

The energy in our food is stored there by other life forms that take it from yet another source: Almost all life on Earth depends on electromagnetic energy that is generated by nuclear fusion in the core of the gas ball that is our Sun. This energy ultimately escapes the Sun as warming, energizing light. Sunlight increases the planet's temperature well above the deep-freezing background of the Universe and supports the growth of plants, thus sustaining the animals that use oxygen and consume food. Plants use the Sun's energy to change electromagnetic bonds in organic compounds that, among other things, enable the growth and ripening of fruits and vegetables. Only weeks after leaving the Sun, the energy may be harvested and enjoyed as food.

The human body is always in a profoundly transient state of being. Accordingly, it is more similar to a relatively constant pattern that allows the perception of a degree of continuity than it is to a static entity with any measure of actual permanence. What outlasts the constant changes is a collection of energy and matter, all of which is steadily replicated to preserve the characteristics of an individual during the span of a lifetime. It will be evident by now that anyone's chronologic age is a practical concept useful for daily life but in fact amounts to nothing more than an illusion. All of this provokes the question: What is the *essence* of the human body, and indeed of life? All life on Earth is integrated with replacement and recycling processes on multiple levels. On the level of the organism, the chemical matter consumed by eating, drinking, and breathing may become integrated for a while to (re)build and power the body, only to be discarded and replaced in due time. As amazing as that is, it represents a narrow view. There is a much larger perspective on life that begins to take shape as we consider the energy on which life depends.

The human body is not solely composed of stardust bound by energy coming from the Sun: It exists by the grace of elements that make up, and are made by, the Universe. Only the body's hydrogen is as old as the Universe. All other elements originate from nuclear fusion inside stars and from explosions that ensued upon the end of their existence. Eventually, gravity trapped enough matter to configure our corner of the Universe. The matter that forms us participates not only in cosmic events but also in organic and inorganic Earth cycles such as continental drift, the water cycle, and the nitrogen cycle. A small amount of matter is added whenever comets hit the Earth or when invisible showers of ultrafast particles enter the atmosphere, and some matter is lost because the atmosphere slowly escapes into space. All life on Earth is composed of elements that are billions of years old, and one of these (hydrogen) has been around as long as the Universe has existed.

It seems a cliché to say that we are made of stardust as if it were a platitude only useful for the lyrics of the 1970s song *Woodstock* by Crosby, Stills, Nash, and Young. But dismissing this notion would negate that human beings are a very small piece of an unfathomably large puzzle, in which the elements that build our bodies are inexorably intertwined with other animals, plants, single-celled organisms, general biological and geological processes, and with the Solar System, the Milky Way Galaxy, and all of the Universe that stretches out to infinity. The diversity in the connections and all their processes is achieved by variation among molecules and the particular assembly of the millions of atoms from which these molecules are made. Life on Earth is based on the elements that are accessible in a form that supports chemical reactions and that are most readily available. Therefore, hydrogen, oxygen, carbon, and nitrogen comprise almost all of our body weight. What the human body is made of, the origin of its components, how it is maintained yet always changing, and how it is intimately connected with everything around it and with the history of time and space may remain obscure most of the time, yet human beings are never separate from a magnificent, all-encompassing, universal ecology. We embody the Universe in a literal sense.

Becoming conscious of the profound interconnectedness of life and the Universe is not inconsequential: That awareness makes it difficult if not impossible to maintain a position along the lines of a strict "self" versus "other," or even "humans" versus "nature." It affects the consideration of other human beings as much as it impacts the views held about other species. It challenges the notion of human existence separate from nature and highlights the futility of unquestioned human superiority. The pretense and hubris of human existence during its relatively minimal presence in the Universe have been revealed for what it is and, if life matters, then actions matter. Life is determined by Earth's climate, which is undergoing unprecedented changes as a result of human activity. During common astronomical and geological cycles, the biosphere has been able to adapt to change by way of stabilizing feedback loops on time scales beyond human lifespans that supported gradual adaptation. At present, however, profound and rapidly unfolding environmental changes may not be curbed prior to irreversible effects. Our own existence is threatened as much as that of the life forms and biological networks that nurture us. Does it matter? The Universe will continue its cycles and recycling, its violent outbursts and subtle changes, with or without human beings. What will it take to awaken to the mystery and wonder? When will humans truly embody the immense privilege of being part of the diversity that is our home?

For Sources and Further Reading

Schrijver, K. (2018). *One of ten billion Earths: How we learn about our planet's past and future from distant exoplanets.* Oxford, UK: Oxford University Press.

Schrijver, K., & Schrijver, I. (2019). *Living with the stars: How the human body is connected to the life cycles of the Earth, the planets, and the stars.* Oxford, UK: Oxford University Press.

2 At Home in Deep Time

Marcia Bjornerud

Geology, with its focus on tangible records of the past, offers a bridge between human experiences of the world and the abstract existential perspectives of philosophy and physics. Becoming familiar with the narratives of natural history – the plots and protagonists that shaped the Earth – can provide a feeling of meaningful "embeddedness" in the cosmos and help us make peace with our embodied selves.

Among the sciences, geology has long been regarded as a second-tier discipline. While institutions of higher education would be considered incomplete without physics, chemistry or biology departments, many colleges and universities have no programs in geology or Earth sciences. Geology – the science certainly most relevant to Earthlings – is not deemed worthy of an Advanced Placement test, or a Nobel Prize. The roots of this attitude are complex. Geology is a relatively young discipline, emerging as a distinct field only in the mid-19th century, and lacking a unifying paradigm (plate tectonics) until the mid-20th. As an applied science that has been propelled largely by the ravenous pursuit of mineral and fossil fuel resources, it has no claim to the cool intellectual purity of physics and chemistry. As a historical, time-and place-bound science, it until recently has not been laboratory-based, carried out instead in the unruly natural world where precision and certainty are rarely attained.

But there may be subtler psychological reasons that geology has been treated as the unloved stepchild within the family of sciences. Apart from its obvious threat to creationist and "young Earth" worldviews, geology is radically transgressive because of its engagement with physical artifacts of the distant past challenges long-held ideas about the nature of matter, the mind/body divide and human exceptionalism.

The very fact that "embodiment" is a topic worthy of academic scrutiny reveals how deeply the illusion of *disembodiment* is rooted in western culture. This conviction is a strange amalgam of ideas – philosophical, theological, scientific, technological – that accreted in an almost physical way (a nice irony) over two millennia in western culture. The foundation of disembodiment is arguably Plato's concept of ethereal "forms" – the view that the true essences of reality hover somewhere beyond our sensory experience of the world and that physical objects we can see or touch are imperfect replicas of these pure and inaccessible entities.

Centuries later, early gnostic Christians regarded all matter as not merely imperfect but as defiled, as the antithesis of the divine. As Christian monks and missionaries sought to purge every vestige of nature worship from the populations they converted, renunciation of the physical and corporeal became a moral doctrine. Old pantheons that were deeply embedded in the landscape were replaced by an abstract, non-localized God and a theology that depicted this world and our bodily selves as corrupt temporary dwellings where souls could lose their way *en route* to heavenly salvation. Although the Copernican and Newtonian revolutions in science later ruffled feathers in the church by displacing the Earth from the center of creation, they did not challenge the more fundamental credo that our minds and souls were something beyond the Earthly realm. The upstart science of geology was the first to do that.

The treatise that announced the arrival of geology as a distinct intellectual endeavor was Sir Charles Lyell's monumental three-volume work *Principles of Geology,* first published between 1830 and 1833. It was a widely distributed and immensely popular work, depicting in vivid prose the emerging evidence for vanished worlds. Charles Darwin took the first volume with him when he left on the voyage of the *HMS Beagle* in 1831, and the book shaped his thinking about how small, incremental changes over time could drive biological evolution. Later, Darwin's ideas would of course unleash the full wrath of those unwilling to see humans as anything less than divinely fashioned creatures.

But Lyell, trained as a lawyer, was a savvy rhetorician. Even as he made the case for an incomprehensibly ancient Earth, he took great care in *Principles of Geology* to draw a sharp line between the physical world whose secrets were being revealed and the intellectual and spiritual domain of humankind. In his analysis of Lyell's influence on Victorian culture (in the journal *Victorian Poetry*, 2004), Michael Tomko considers Alfred Tennyson's *In Memoriam* – an elegiac meditation on mortality in the context of materialist science. Tomko notes, "Lyell's work is often read only as a source of overwhelming anxiety for Tennyson, as a baldly atheistic list of theories or a dreadful set of facts, rather than as a complex, culturally aware, religiously astute text" (p. 114). Whether or not Lyell himself believed it, he intentionally downplayed the potential psychological threat posed by the new geological worldview by "introducing a strict, impassable division between the natural and spiritual [which] provides a secure, interior, spiritual realm but also effectively eviscerates the body" (Tomko, p. 115).

Lyell's tactical maneuver of keeping the human mind at a safe remove from physical phenomena was temporarily successful – allowing geology to enjoy two decades of unconditional love – because the first editions of *Principles of Geology* did not directly address biological evolution nor, especially, human origins. But Darwin's *Origin of Species* (1859), *Descent of Man* (1871), and his lesser known but prescient *The Expression of the Emotions in Man [sic] and Animals* (1872) began to perforate Lyell's "impassable division" by revealing how our bodies, minds, and behaviors can be traced to animal ancestry. Today, modern advances in archeology, genetics, neuroscience, psychology, and medicine make it increasingly difficult to argue for any clear line between our physical and mental selves. It is appearing more and more likely that we too are mere matter.

But perhaps a neo-Lyellian geological perspective can help us to embrace at last our embodied nature. As Lyell recognized, the salient lesson of the geologic record is the power of time to alter, erode, innovate, transmute, and recreate. If we feel diminished by the idea of having arisen from mere matter, maybe it is because we have underestimated matter.

Perhaps we don't understand that 4.6 billion years ago, mere matter from stellar explosions coalesced to form a new star with fuel to last 10 billion years, illuminating a swarm of nascent planets. Or that the mere matter in one of those planets separated into a rocky mantle and an iron core, which in turn began to convect. Or that this roiling core, mere metal, soon began to generate a powerful magnetic field that has ever after shielded the planet from cosmic rays; meanwhile, the churning mantle refined itself through melting and remelting, yielding magmas of basalt and then granite, laying the foundations for mere continents. And that volcanoes conveying this molten rock to the surface also exhaled mere water and carbon dioxide that formed a mere ocean and atmosphere.

And maybe we have not appreciated that soon after that, some mere matter began to reproduce and continuously modify itself as it spread out across the mere planet. And that when the Earth was still in its childhood, some of those self-replicating organisms developed the sophisticated habit of photosynthesis. Using volcano breath and the light of the sun, they infused the atmosphere with free oxygen and have been feeding all the rest of us mere Earthlings for the subsequent 3.8 billion years. If we feel debased by the idea we evolved from microbes, then we misjudge the astonishing technological prowess and versatility of prokaryotes – and deny the fact that the teeming microbiome of bacterial cells in our bodies outnumbers our own animal cells. The lone ego is an illusion; each of us is plural, multitudes.

The rock record makes obvious how our bodies are part of a continuum from raw Earth to endlessly ramifying Life, an unbroken chain of living organisms that stretches back to the early days of the planet. How marvelous to know that our bones – minerals made of calcium and phosphorous, derived from rocks – can be mapped one-to-one onto those of almost every other vertebrate from amphibians to zebras. How amazing to realize that our blood is a distant memory of seawater. How good to feel in our marrow that we are fully native to this old, verdant, resilient Earth. Any alienation we feel is self-inflicted; any existential torment we may suffer over our origins amounts to ignorance and disrespect for our forebears.

Geology is a strange blend of the pragmatic and philosophical. It is responsible for more than its share of environmental sins, but it also offers breathtaking vistas of vast timespans. While other sciences, particularly astrophysics, offer glimpses of the cosmic, their focus is on objects too abstract and far away for us to grasp in any literal way. Modern physics – the science of the physical world – is largely non-physical, immaterial, theoretical.

The practice of geology is, in contrast, very physical, concerned with tangible objects – rocks, fossils, mountains, ice – and involves direct bodily engagement with the landscape. While laboratory sciences strive to keep the bodies of investigators separate from the objects of study, with white coats and enclosed experiments, geologists must enter into the terrain to fathom it. In fieldwork, geologists develop a visceral sense of scale by traversing topography on foot; pace length and eye height are still used as measuring tools in creating rough maps. And one's evolving understanding of the geological backstory of a particular area is inevitably entangled with personal experience of that place – the weather, one's companions, where the group paused for lunch.

Although not everyone can or should become a geologist, geologic habits of mind – a sense of temporal proportion, an instinct for our place in Earth's story – may serve all Earthlings as an antidote to the dangerous illusion of disembodiment. Environmental misconduct and existential malaise both stem from a distorted sense of who we are as a species in the context of the natural world. Modern anomie arises out of disconnection from history and natural history, and it is intensified by the loss of physical engagement with the world owing to our increasingly virtual interactions with people and things.

The remedy is to reclaim our pre-Platonic kinship with the Earth and all its denizens, animate and inanimate. Learning the narratives of natural history and getting to know the protagonists by name can provide a feeling of meaningful embodiment and embeddedness in the cosmos. This is the essential premise of Aldo Leopold's "Land Ethic" (in his 1949 *Sand County Almanac*) which

> enlarges the boundaries of the community to include soils, waters, plants, and animals, or collectively: the land… it changes the role of *Homo sapiens* from conqueror of the land-community to plain member and citizen of it. It implies respect for his fellow-members, and also respect for the community as such.
>
> (p. 204)

As Robin Wall Kimmerer writes (in *Orion Magazine*, 2017), a first step toward achieving such a shift in perception is to adopt a conscious "grammar of animacy": "Kin are ripening in the fields; kin are nesting under the eaves; kin are flying south for the winter, come back soon. Our words can be an antidote to human exceptionalism, to unthinking exploitation, an antidote to loneliness."

Thinking like a geologist – or a botanist or ecologist – can simultaneously ground us and elevate us. Paradoxically, these Earthbound, very physical sciences yield transcendent insights. Matter, both living and non-living, has accomplished many astonishing things over the past four billion years. Our own material minds have now learned to read the archives of those eons. Why would we even consider disavowing such a long and distinguished heritage of embodiment?

For Sources and Further Reading

Bjornerud, M. (2006). *Reading the rocks: The autobiography of the earth.* New York: Basic Books.

Bjornerud, M. (2018). *Timefulness: How thinking like a geologist can help save the world.* Princeton, NJ: Princeton University Press.

Kimmerer, R. W. (2015). *Braiding sweetgrass: Indigenous wisdom, scientific knowledge and the teaching of plants.* Minneapolis, MN: Milkweed Editions.

Von Humboldt, A. (2014). *Views of nature* (M. Person, S. Jackson, & L. D. Walls, Trans.). Chicago, IL: University of Chicago Press (Original work published in 1807).

3   The Secrets of Life
The Vital Roles of RNA Networks and Viruses

Luis P. Villarreal and Guenther Witzany

Viruses and related infectious genetic parasites are the most abundant biological agents on this planet. They invade all cellular organisms, are key agents in the generation of adaptive and innate immune systems, and drive nearly all regulatory processes within living cells.

The lives of humans and other large animals might seem distantly connected to bits of subcellular agents such as viruses and similar genetic parasites. Their fates, however, are intimately entwined. A typical human body contains more microbes than human cells, and incorporation of retroviruses and related genetic parasites into DNA accounts for at least half of the human genome. Understanding human life requires understanding life – and, specifically, communication and cooperation – on the tiniest of scales.

The modern philosophy of communication makes clear that natural languages or codes emerge through population-based interactions. Any natural language or code is the result of social interaction in which biotic populations can communicate, to coordinate and organize common goals. No natural language speaks itself, and no natural code codes itself. Therefore, there must be competent agents to generate language signs or codes (including the genetic code), combine signs to sequences based on grammar rules, designate something by content-coherent rules (*semantics*), and use signs in communicative interactions in real-life circumstances in a context-dependent way (*pragmatics*).

The study of ribonucleic acid (RNA) and viruses (*virology*) has illuminated how and why a genetic code emerged, evolved, and plays essential roles in all living agents on this planet. Examining the genetic code together with current RNA biology and virology reveals that RNA and viruses *cooperate*. In addition, scholarly cooperation between virology and philosophy of communication creates a new perspective to better understand life, its complexity, and its evolution. Cooperation – not selfishness – provides the key to understanding the secret of life. In this essay, we describe some of the most important themes of this cooperation.

Falsified Key Assumptions of the 20th Century

Several key assumptions of the last century serve as a basis for a picture of life, a picture which underlies most research projects and convictions on emergence of disease, and therefore underlies investments in the development of new drugs. Those assumptions no longer hold up against scientific knowledge:

- The *one gene-one protein hypothesis* has been falsified through *epigenetics,* which demonstrates that *varieties* of different proteins can be translated out of *identical* genetic information.
- The idea that *noncoding deoxyribonucleic acid (DNA) is junk* has been falsified by demonstrating that noncoding regions assemble noncoding RNAs that *play essential roles* in transcription, translation, and an abundance of gene regulations.
- The *central dogma of molecular biology* (DNA →RNA → Protein) has been falsified by demonstrating that RNAs that *regulate gene expression* may be coded into DNA or, together with proteins, change genetic identities.
- The idea that *evolution results entirely from random genetic variations and biological selection* has been falsified. Genetic variations have been assumed to be caused mainly by replication errors. Today's genomic analysis reveals that besides error-based mutations that may cause disease, *most beneficial genetic variations are the result of persistent viruses and their defective relatives* such as transposons and retrotransposons.

A New Picture of Life

Exposing the deep flaws in those key assumptions has set the stage for a new picture of life, a view grounded in radically new understandings of the roles DNA, RNA, and viruses.

DNA Serves Only as Habitat (the "House"),
RNAs Act as Inhabitants

For decades, DNA has been the central focus of efforts to understand the determinants of evolution and development of all organisms (except RNA viruses). DNA sequencing promised knowledge about which genes are responsible for features, capabilities, and disease in all life forms, including humans. Genetic manipulation as well as genetic engineering in breeding and gene therapy mainly looked at DNA as a toolbox of molecular bricks. This focus persists today. But DNA is only a relatively stable storage medium. DNA is inhabited by RNA parasites with a variety of group-behavioral motifs and goals. Given the more active and dynamic role for RNA in living organisms, we should consider RNAs as the living agents and DNA as their habitat. From this perspective, RNAs can be seen as open space invaders.

Evolution of Genetic Novelty by RNA Groups

How do RNA parasites exceed their physio-chemical boundaries to transform life? Even at this subcellular level, a key principle operates: Group membership is crucial for living networks to emerge. Beyond DNA and RNA base *pairs* (e.g., the bases guanine and cytosine forming a G–C base pair), RNA has *multi-base* sequences at the end of the molecule (*stem loops*). Single RNA stem loops interact with other molecules in a physico-chemical way without features that are *biotic* (i.e. characteristic of life forms). But any interaction involving one RNA molecule can involve many other, different RNA molecules. These interactions are building blocks of life.

When the density of RNA stem loops reaches a critical mass, *biological selection* emerges. Crucially, within biological selection of RNA stem loops, a core of historic *behavioral motifs* is ever present. These motifs include *parasitism*, splicing (*ligation*), splitting (*cleavage*), and group building. The motifs reflect and shape genetic and group identities, a process of *dynamic self-directed learning*. Initial learning requires learning *self-identity*.

How does self-identity emerge in RNA group building? Single RNA stem loops join groups, and group membership is the prerequisite for self/non-self-differentiation. To survive, RNA stem loop replicators must assemble in groups that dynamically generate group identity. RNA stem loops are ligated to other stem loops that fit into the group identity and cleave those that do not fit. Self-ligation of RNA stem loops forms a module-pool that participates in many cooperative interactions, leading to ribozymes and the capacity for RNA cleavage. Interestingly, the genetic identity of RNA stem loops groups may change quickly in response to environmental necessities, and formerly rejected stem loops may later fit well into the group (or vice versa).

The ongoing, dynamic nature of group identity and selection also is expressed in how infectious RNA stem loops operate via RNA groups. These extended groups are called *quasi-species consortia*. Quasi-species consortia produce and depend on diversity; diversity is not an "error" but rather a fundamental property of the groups. RNA stem loop variations play a crucial role in building quasi-species consortia: Especially the binding-prone single-stranded loops and bulges interact and build new groups with distinct identities. An RNA group with a specific identity may cooperate with other RNA groups in building networks. Importantly, RNA groups retain memory of past events via minorities, so their survival does not depend on selection of a "Fittest Type" but rather on an ongoing process of selection for heterogeneity.

The evolution of early RNA-based life, then, was *communal*: Cooperation is key, and RNA group behavior generated the origin of the genetic code, a real natural language.

Viruses Are Masters in the Editing of Genetic Codes

Viruses and related infectious genetic parasites are the most abundant biological agents on this planet. They vastly outnumber cellular life forms, invade all cellular organisms, and serve as key agents in the generation of adaptive and innate immune systems. The invasion strategy that results in persistence within host genomes (*genomic parasitism*) provides novel evolutionary genetic identities that were not present prior to the invasion. The remnants of persistent viral infection events include transposable elements (transposons and retrotransposons) in the host genome which all share a repetitive sequence syntax. Even highly fragmented parasitic genetic elements can create new RNA networks that are directly involved in gene regulation found in all organisms. When viruses cooperate with hosts, they are the *only* living entities that share all variants of genetic sequence syntax from RNA to DNA, from single-stranded to double-stranded, and from repetitive to nonrepetitive sequences.

One cooperative motif that is successful for invading DNA habitats is the *addiction module*. It is the main behavioral motif that interconnects communication of RNA groups, viruses, and cell-based organisms and accounts for the persistence of viral elements. Competing genetic parasites, together with a host immune system, build counterbalancing modules and genetic counterregulation (e.g., toxin/antitoxin, restriction/modification, insertion/deletion, etc.). In such a counterbalanced module, viruses do not harm the host.

Host organisms depend on such counterbalancing agents and are in that sense "addicted" to them: If the counterbalance is disturbed, then one part of the addiction module (e.g., a toxin) may become dominant and harm the host. Most disease results from addiction modules being out of counterbalanced control.

Thus, like stem-loop RNA consortia, viruses are a force for ancient, recent, and contemporary life. They are natural genome editors with core competences including innovation, integration, regulation, and setting the stage for further selection (*exaptation*). Wherever viruses exist and interact with hosts (the *virosphere*), persistent viral life strategies are beneficial for their hosts. The strategies result from special group behavioral motifs ever present in the virosphere such as cooperation (in addiction modules, to reach persistent balance) and collective actions of dispersed defective viruses in infection and integration processes.

RNA Networks, Viruses, and Cells Constitute Life

Cellular life means metabolizing entities with membranes that ensure genetic identity and rejection of parasites via immune systems. Cellular life characterizes organisms from bacteria, amoeba, and fungi to animals and plants. Before cellular life emerged, RNA networks replicated. Although cellular life is a result of RNA consortia interactions, genetic parasites such as viruses shaped cellular life through constant infection, innovation, immune function, and selection via reproduction. Capsid-encoding viruses and cellular life may have originated in a complementary way, but viruses undoubtedly had their roots in the depth of the RNA world and represent many genes and sequences never found in the cellular world, which indicates a pre-cellular origin.

A Social Science Perspective on RNA Networks, Viruses, and Cells

The new concept of *quasi-species consortia* primarily focuses on RNA interactions together with viruses that represent groups with identity, which means they differ from groups that do not share that identity. This social science perspective looks at RNA societies which share a self/nonself-identification competence. Group behavior of RNA networks including viruses (i.e., their infection competence) has several motifs to integrate foreign stem loop groups that fit into present group identity or to expand group identity for novel context-relevant functions.

The main objective remains group identity, which is constituted not by uniform members, clones, or similar low-level variations but mainly of very different members such as former competing agents and rejected minorities. The quasi-species consortia are characterized by different agents that compete, are rejected, or remain as defectives. Such consortia also present a selection profile: A consortium regulates gene expression, creates epigenetic marks, and generates new, evolutionarily relevant nucleotide sequences, all of which is subject to selection. Each member serves a counterbalancing function and can react to specific circumstances in ways that other members cannot; therefore, a consortium integrates competing RNA stem loop groups in context-relevant ways. The two subunits which form a *ribosome* (RNA with associated proteins), for instance, have a group identity very different from the identities of other large RNA stem loop groups; each has its own evolutionary history and original function, and each may integrate or reject other foreign RNA stem loops. A group identity arises with this integration/rejection (self/nonself) behavioral motif. They are integrated via addiction module function into a DNA-stored essential tool, for all cellular life.

The social science perspective on RNA biology and virology has more explanatory power than previous theories because it can integrate diverse motifs of RNA stem loop groups into a consortial biotic behavior that formerly was described only in a physio-chemical realm of individual Fittest Types. Further, what has been explained in the past by replication errors – namely variations – is now an essential feature of RNA stem loop group behavior to generate unforeseeable, newly created forms, functions, and structures of RNA groups. To call this productivity "error" now looks like an outdated error of the last century.

Conclusion

Virology and philosophy of communication together present a new perspective to look at life as a whole and on life in all its details based on the most recent empirical and philosophical knowledge. If we look at key features of life as we know it on our planet, including immune systems, replication, transcription, translation, and repair in all its steps and substeps, we can justify the conclusion that all these features and properties are the result of evolutionary innovations caused, generated, and introduced by viruses, RNA consortia, and other genetic parasites. These infectious agents are the innovators of

RNA stem loop group interactions of all life. They insert and delete, adapt, modify, and, most importantly, counterbalance competing genetic identities. They cooperate, edit genetic codes, and are at the basis of the secrets of life – including human life.

For Sources and Further Reading

Villarreal, L. P. (2015). Can virolution help us understand recent human evolution? In V. Kolb (Ed.), *Astrobiology: An evolutionary approach* (pp. 441–472). Boca Raton, FL: CRC Press.

Villarreal, L. P., & Witzany, G. (2010). Viruses are essential agents within the roots and stem of the tree of life. *Journal of Theoretical Biology, 262,* 698–710.

Villarreal, L. P., & Witzany, G. (2019). That is life: Communicating RNA networks from viruses and cells in continuous interaction. *Annals of the New York Academy of Sciences, 1447,* 5–20.

Webpages: https://www.researchgate.net/profile/Luis_Villarreal3, www.biocommunication.at

4 A Brief History of Death

Sheldon Solomon

North and south; hot and cold; life and death. All common examples of polar opposites. You cannot be heading north and south at the same time. Your coffee cannot be hot and cold at the same time. And surely you cannot be alive and dead at the same time. Or can you? The distinction between life and death is not as simple or obvious as it appears to be.

Biologists generally maintain that death likely originated with the advent of life and is necessary to maintaining life (see, for example, Volk & Sagan, 2009). But what is death? When is one dead? Is death irreversible? Theologians, philosophers, biologists, and physicians have pondered these questions since antiquity and, for the most part, there is little dispute regarding responses to these queries for all forms of life except humans. Death is the irreversible cessation of an organism's vital functions. Logically, then, life and death are mutually exclusive – one is either alive or dead. Moreover, death marks the permanent end of life. Death is terminal, literally and figuratively – no round trips or do-overs.

For humans, however, these questions have always been both more pressing and more complicated, in that an unintended consequence of our vast intelligence is the realization that death is inevitable and can occur at any time for reasons that cannot always be anticipated or controlled. "As a naked fact," philosopher Susanne Langer observed, "that realization is unacceptable...Nothing, perhaps, is more comprehensible than that people...would rather reject than accept the idea of death as an inevitable close of their brief earthly careers." Consequently, throughout history humans have been ardently devoted to understanding, forestalling, reversing, and transcending death.

One approach to death transcendence is via religious belief systems in which death is viewed as a transition to a more pleasant and enduring afterlife. Chinese nobles, following the proverb "treat death as life," buried their servants, artisans, concubines, and soldiers alive with them when they died. Egyptian royalty and nobility were entombed in magnificent pyramids, stocked with clothing, furniture, toiletries, food and drink, and life-size wooden boats for transport to the netherworld. In the Islamic tradition, the afterlife is located in the heavenly Gardens of Delight, where miraculous trees are made of silver or gold, and the dead are resurrected in perpetually young bodies, untarnished by pubic hair or mucous. Virtually, all religions also embrace the concept of souls, although their specific nature varies considerably across time and space. Some souls are physical entities, ranging from full-sized shadows to miniature replicas of the body; other souls are immaterial. Souls render the prospect of immortality feasible by enabling humans to perceive themselves as potentially detachable from their corporeal containers.

Humans have also diligently attempted to forestall death by not dying. Throughout history, people searched for sacred places where they would reputedly live forever: The Isles of the Blest for the Greeks; The Land of Living Men, featuring a race of giants who never aged or died for the Teutons. Magical fruits, seeds, and waters could also preclude dying: for the Celts of Western Europe, eating enchanted foods or using a magic vessel found at the Land of Youth; an eternal spring that eliminated sickness, age, or death on the Japanese island of Horaisan; the Hindu Pool of Youth; the Hebrew River of Immortality. In China, Tao alchemists spent centuries trying to produce "drugs of no death." (See Cave, 2012, and Solomon et al., 2015, for more on literal immortality.)

Despite these earnest and persistent efforts to overcome death, it was quite evident that every human being who had ever been alive ultimately apparently perished at some point. This observation led to equally tenacious exertions to determine precisely when death occurs, in part to ensure that individuals were not declared to be deceased prematurely. When is one dead? As Dick Teresi described in his 2012 book, *The Undead*, how death is determined has changed over time. His chronology, in brief, is as follows: Historically, the determination depended on the organ or body part deemed necessary for the body to remain operational. For the ancient Egyptians and Greeks, the heart was the primary organ of life, so death was when one's heart stopped beating. For the Hebrews and Christians, one was dead when respiration ceased: no breath = no life; the Hebrews further stipulated that the only unequivocal indication of death was bodily purification.

To ensure that people were not too hastily abandoned, interred, or cremated, ancient Greeks cut off a finger from a putative corpse; Plato recommended waiting for three days before burial. The Romans put bodies in a warm bath or rubbed them with hot water; they also practiced *conclamation*: summoning the person by name three times. In Europe in the Middle Ages, vigils for dead neighbors served to certify that the superficially deceased were genuinely dead. Despite such precautions, by the mid-1700s, compilations of accounts of premature burials made it quite clear that it was quite unclear at times how to determine who was unequivocally dead. Medical technologies, including artificial respiration, smelling salts, and electric shocks, were increasingly deployed to make such decisions, leading Ben Franklin to observe in 1773, "It appears that the doctrines of life and death in general are yet but little understood."

The progressive reliance on medical technologies to determine the time of death was accompanied by a shift from cardiovascular and respiratory criteria to brain death as the basis for such decisions. Scientists and physicians emphasized the distinction between basic organic (e.g., cardiac and pulmonary) bodily functions common to most life forms, and sophisticated brain-based processes that engender sensation and volition. With the advent of ventilators, fatally brain-damaged people could continue breathing while their hearts kept beating. Are they dead? What about people in a persistent vegetative state, who, for months or even years, show no signs of higher brain function and seem completely unresponsive to psychological and physical stimuli? Are they dead? By the 20th century, and to this day, irreversible coma, or brain death, marks the end of life, rather than the cessation of bodily functions per se. People are technically dead, then, when they are no longer "themselves," even if all of their other vital organs are fully or partially functional.

This conception of human death is potentially problematic, however. First, the Ad Hoc Committee of the Harvard Medical School to Examine the Definition of Brain Death, which concluded in 1968 that anyone who had a "permanently nonfunctioning brain" was technically dead, was contemporaneous with burgeoning improvements in organ transplant technology. Perhaps, some argued, well-intentioned efforts by transplant surgeons to forestall the death of those in need of organs were, literally, at the expense of seriously ill potential donors, who were nevertheless not-quite-dead when they were declared deceased in order to harvest their organs to maintain the organs' viability for transplant purposes. Maybe this would be morally inconsequential for brain-dead patients in a truly irreversible coma. There are, however, documented instances of people declared brain dead being resuscitated, even while they are being prepared to have their organs harvested for transplant.

Moreover, other seemingly brain-dead patients are actually quite alive and alert, despite being severely incapacitated and unable to express themselves directly. For example, Kate Bainbridge was in a vegetative state for almost two years after a 1997 bout of encephalitis when a neuropsychologist conducted a PET scan to assess her intellectual capacity – a procedure that was undertaken primarily to give her family hope. Quite unexpectedly, the scan revealed normal levels of intellectual functioning, obscured by Kate being paralyzed and unable to communicate at the time. After regaining limited movement, and communicating by pointing to letters on a board, Kate expressed concern that she might have been mistaken for a brain-dead organ donor had she not had the PET scan, saying "they should never let people die without assessing them properly."

Near death experiences (NDEs) during a coma or cardiac arrest pose a slightly different challenge to the notion of brain death as the primary criterion for determining when one is technically dead. The most frequently reported core elements of NDEs, which are quite consistent across cultures and independent of religious beliefs, are: awareness of being dead during the experience, pleasant feelings, out-of-body experiences, perceptions of a warm and bright light, encounters with deceased people or other beings, and the sight of a heavenly or hellish landscape. Some physicians and psychologists explain the core elements of NDEs as dream-like hallucinations. What, however, is the neuroanatomical locus of such experiences if the person having the NDE is technically brain dead at the time? Additionally, there are documented cases of veridical experiences during NDEs – that is, brain-dead patients reporting out-of-body experiences including accurate descriptions of, for instance, hospital emergency rooms and conversations by doctors and nurses at the time the patient was technically dead. Such experiences imply that a functional brain (as clinically assessed) is not necessary for non-hallucinatory states of awareness, which seemingly calls into question the claim that brain-dead people are truly dead.

Although scientific progress generally tends to clarify our understanding of complex phenomena, improvements in medical technology since antiquity have made unequivocal determination of human death murkier. The time between when legal dictates or social customs deem one dead and when physicians and neuroscientists deem one dead has lengthened. In humankind's early days, the temporal gap between being apparently dead and being summarily disposed or ceremonially interred was fairly immediate. The gap grew a bit over time as it became evident that people could be declared dead but then subsequently recover hours, or even days later, perhaps from freezing or drowning. Now the gap is months or even years, given documented instances of brain-dead patients' spontaneous recoveries and seemingly brain-dead patients who are actually mentally alert and totally sensate.

This temporal gap will likely increase in the future as medical technology becomes more sophisticated, and humans persist in our species-defining quest to forestall and ultimately overcome death. Although most people have abandoned expeditions seeking sacred places with magical waters and fruits to extend life indefinitely, humans have by no means forsaken other approaches to remaining undead for as long as possible. As described in the Immortality Institute's 2004 volume, *The Scientific Conquest of Death*, modern "immortalists" strive to delineate the biological underpinnings of aging so as to discover the optimal combination of vitamins and nutritional supplements to extend our natural life span. People now have their bodies frozen after they "die," in anticipation of future technological developments enabling them to be resuscitated. Most cryogenically preserved humans are decapitated first; only the head and brain is frozen, in accord with advice on the Alcor Life Extension Foundation website that "it makes no sense to preserve...a large mass of aged, diseased tissue that may very well be completely replaced during revival anyway." If a presently frozen head is reanimated in a few 1,000 years, was the person ever totally dead millennia ago?

Meanwhile, human body parts are now routinely replaced with more durable alternatives: knees, hips, shoulders, iron rod vertebrae, and even plastic hearts. Innovations in the works include computer-assisted intelligence and nanobots – tiny robots to monitor and regulate digestive processes and serve as miniature trash compactors to replace bowel functions. Some futurists favor "non-invasive static uploading" to store all of the information in a human brain on a computer cloud as a back-up in case of memory loss, including one's sense of self, during bodily maintenance or repair. Others question the wisdom of returning one's knowledge and identity to a physical body. Why not abandon a respiring carbon-based embodiment entirely and "relocate" to a sturdier and long-lived silicon-based corporeal foundation? In what sense will silicon-based entities be alive? What will constitute dying under such conditions?

"Life," as the saying goes, "goes on." Death too, although what we mean by *living* and *dying* may change in interesting and unforeseen ways in the future...

For Sources and Further Reading

Cave, S. (2012). *Immortality: The quest to live forever and how it drives civilization.* New York: Crown Publishers.

Immortality Institute (Ed.). (2004). *The scientific conquest of death: Essays on infinite lifespans.* Wausau, WI: Libros en Red.

Langer, S. K. (1982). *Mind: An essay on human feeling* (Vol. III). Baltimore, MD: Johns Hopkins Press.

Smith, A. (1863/1892). *Dreamthorp, a book of essays written in the country.* London, UK: Oxford University Press.

Solomon, S., Greenberg, J., & Pyszczynski, T. (2015). *The worm at the core: On the role of death in life.* New York: Random House.

Teresi, D. (2012). *The undead: Organ harvesting, the ice water test, beating-heart cadavers—How medicine is blurring the line between life and death.* New York: Pantheon Books.

Volk, T., & Sagan, D. (2009). *Death and sex.* Chelsea, VT: Chelsea Green Publishing.

Part II

Engaging

How does a body shape its dynamic engagement with the world in which it is immersed? In what ways are bodies physical manifestations of those dynamic engagements? What is the relation of an active body to agency, learning, and noetic experience? The essays in this section take up these questions, each utilizing a unique perspective on environmentally embedded deployments and transformations of the body, from gene expression to reading pleasure.

5 Attentive Bodies

Epigenetic Processes and Concepts of Human Being

Samantha Frost

The patterned logic of epigenetic processes suggests that they are a non-neurological means by which bodies pay attention to the world. This possibility disrupts some of the central categories that thinkers in the West have used for conceptualizing embodied subjectivity.

Epigenetics research shows that bodies are responsive genetically to experiences of their environments, which is to say that the ways our bodies grow and function are deeply and durably susceptible to the places we live and to our modes of living. While epigenetic processes unfold as biochemical changes in molecules and cells, research shows that the factors that provoke them are not only the biochemistry of nutrition and toxins but also and sometimes more profoundly the effects of living with racial and sexual discrimination and economic deprivation. Consequently, when epigenetic processes change how our bodies use genes, they infuse the very matter of biological life with the effects of social and political life, shaping not just how bodies work but how they develop, grow, and persist over time. Understandably, epigenetic processes transform medical and scientific accounts of biology and health. But in showing how the material dimensions of biological bodies are socially and politically formed – and thus in showing that there is no moment in which a biological body could be said to be pure or unformed by social and political life – epigenetic processes also demand theoretical work on some of the fundamental concepts in the history of Western thought. They demand that we consider what epigenetic processes mean for our understanding of what human beings are and of how humans live in their worlds.

Maurizio Meloni (2019, this volume) observes that the notion that biologies are "impressionable" has historical precedent in the

Hippocratic and humoral traditions of medicine. Here, different facets of the natural, climatic, nutritional, and built environment were considered to affect the development of health and personality. What is distinctive in the re-emergence of impressionable biologies today is that in epigenetic processes, the body is not passively subject to its environment but instead is actively engaged in its own responsive transformations. Georges Canguilhem (2008[1965]) observes that in recent history, bodily phenotypes – or historically specific living bodies – have been considered as changeable in the course of engaging with the vagaries of the lived environment: famine, climate, disease, or conflict might affect the health and function of phenotypic bodies. In contrast, the genotype – bodies considered as repositories of genetic code – was thought to be protected from all these, preserving the instructions for the construction of a new, unalloyed body each generation. But as Lappé and Landecker (2015) explain, epigenetics research suggests that experiences of unequal social relations, nutrition, toxins, poverty, and other forms of stress affect the shape and structure of chromatin, which is the conglomeration of proteins and macromolecules that bind DNA together and makes genes accessible or inaccessible to transcription. Epigenetic processes transform chromatin so profoundly that the genome can no longer be conceived as a timeless sourcebook for the making of each generation. As Lappé and Landecker remark, "time and history have come into the genome itself" (p. 117).

It is clear that the forms of marking, memory, and biological adjustment that are seen in epigenetic processes require a conceptual reworking of the relationship between genomes, bodies, and environments. Here, I argue that if we trace the logic of the unfolding of epigenetic transformations, they seem to evince both *anticipation* and *intentionality*. The anticipatory and intentional characteristics of epigenetic processes suggest, in turn, that we might conceive of epigenetic processes as a form of paying attention.

Zaneta Thayer and Christopher Kuzawa (2011) argue that epigenetic processes mark living bodies' experiences, forming a kind of memory. For example, nutritional stress in neonatal and early postnatal life can provoke epigenetic transformations that affect metabolic health later in life as well as in subsequent generations. Likewise, psychosocial stress in the form of workplace and social inequality or extreme duress (as in the experience of Holocaust survivors) provoke epigenetic transformations that affect stress physiology and health for several generations. Christopher Kuzawa and

Elizabeth Sweet (2009, cited in Thayer & Kuzawa, 2011) similarly observe that the stresses generated by chronic daily experiences of racism provoke epigenetic processes that change biological systems so that those that deal with stress are highly sensitive and those that enhance immunity are depressed. They argue that this combination of transformations helps explain the heightened vulnerability to cardiovascular disease observed in African American communities.

Now, although epigenetic processes can be helpfully conceived as a kind of memory of experience, if we follow the patterned logic of those processes, they can also be seen as a kind of anticipation. Epigenetic processes shape the ways genes are used to build and rebuild bodies on a daily basis. When they prompt bodies to rebuild to be more sensitively responsive to the stresses of experiencing racism (for instance), the transformations in gene use they promote are not an effect of *recovery* from the past experience (as in the case of a scar, for instance). Instead, in making stress response systems more highly sensitive, epigenetic processes are *preparing* the body to be ready for further experience of racism. In preparing the body to be ready, epigenetic processes *functionally anticipate* a recurrence of the experiences that prompted them.

This figuration of epigenetic processes as not just a form of memory (a record of the past) but also anticipatory (concerned with the future) brings to the foreground another feature, which is their intentionality. The concept of intentionality in philosophy is used to denote that a claim, a thought, or a perception is "about" an object. For example, one might describe my action of swatting a fly as intentional because my arm moves vis-à-vis the fly buzzing irritatingly by my head. In other words, the action is "about" the fly. In the case of epigenetic processes, we could say that they exhibit a *mediated* form of intentionality, but intentionality nonetheless. When epigenetic processes enable a body to prepare to experience something again, they exhibit the functional presumption (the anticipation) that the experience will happen again. This functional presumption concerns the conditions of the world that generate the experience; it is a presumption that previously experienced conditions in the world will repeat or recur. So, epigenetic processes are intentional in that they are *about* the world of experience. This "aboutness" is a mediated form of intentionality in that epigenetic processes are prompted not directly by experience but instead by the body's response to its experience – its response to its response to the world. But nonetheless, it is a form of intentionality.

This combination of anticipation and intentionality is important because it suggests that living bodies are not passively receiving inputs about the material and social conditions of existence. According to the logic of epigenetic processes laid out here, in anticipating a future experience in a specific futural form of the world, bodies are paying attention to the world at a molecular and cellular level. Indeed, this is the main claim of this essay: Epigenetic processes are a means by which bodies pay attention to the world. And significantly, even though epigenetic processes may be shaped by perception, self-reflection, and imagination – as claimed by Bradley Turnwald and colleagues (2019) – the form of paying attention that they appear to embody is not managed by the neurological system. That is to say, epigenetic processes appear to be a non-neurological form of attention. It is difficult to give imaginative or conceptual form to a kind of attention that is not managed by the neurological system: How to think it? Indeed, what is theoretically fascinating is that this form of attention suggests that the matter of the body is generating meaning, is making meaning of the world in ways that have generally been reserved for complex neurological systems and creatures capable of linguistic representation.

In sum, as molecular scale attentive responses to experiences of the social and material world, epigenetic processes represent a complete disruption of the long-standing distinction between the raw, material, animal processes of the body oriented only towards survival and the purportedly more elevated processes bound up with taste and aesthetics, habit, movement, acculturation, thought, and language. In disrupting this distinction between matter and meaning – a distinction at the very foundation of Western thought – epigenetic processes also throw into disarray a host of other categorical distinctions that have organized thinking about people and politics in the Western political tradition. Cause and effect, active and passive, subject and object, subjective and objective: All of these distinctions rest on the distinction between matter and meaning, and they scaffold the ways that people in the West think about what makes humans human and what makes political life distinct from natural life. If we can trace out the successive conceptual disruptions that are provoked by our increasing knowledge of epigenetic processes, we may develop concepts that defamiliarize our understanding of democratic political cultures and that point to unexpected possibilities for political transformation.

For Sources and Further Reading

Canguilhem, G. (2008[1965]). *Knowledge of life* (S. Geroulanos & D. Ginsburg, Trans.). New York: Fordham University Press (Original work published in 1965).

Fox, M., Thayer, Z. M., & Wadhwa, P. (2017). Acculturation and health: The moderating role of sociocultural context. *American Anthropologist, 119*(3), 405–421.

Frost, S. (2016). *Biocultural creatures: Towards a new theory of the human.* Durham: Duke University Press.

Lappé, M., & Landecker, H. (2015). How the genome got a lifespan. *New Genetics and Society, 34*(2), 152–176.

Meloni, M. (2019). *Impressionable biologies: From the archeology of plasticity to the sociology of epigenetics.* New York: Routledge.

Thayer, Z. M., & Kuzawa, C. W. (2011). Biological memories of past environments: Epigenetic pathways to health disparities. *Epigenetics, 6*(7), 798–803.

Turnwald, B., Parker Goyer, J., Boles, D. Z., Silder, A., Delp, S. L., & Crum, A. J. (2019). Learning one's genetic risk changes physiology independent of actual genetic risk. *Nature Human Behavior, 3*, 48–56.

6 Uncovering the Living Body

Bodies and Agents in the Cognitive Sciences

Fred Keijzer

As long as the concept "embodiment" remains tied to the widely applicable notion of "agent," it will remain insufficiently constrained and kept away from the empirical foundation that living bodies provide for the cognitive sciences.

Usually, we keep our bodies covered. Physically, we wrap them in textiles, and conceptually we hide them under layers of interpretation and meaning. In contrast to the physical ones, the conceptual wrappings are not so easily removed or changed. They consist of enduring encrustations that shape our perceptions and thoughts about our bodies – and ourselves – in more permanent ways. The case that I will address here concerns the concept of "agent" and the way it influences our view of the body within the cognitive sciences.

Starting about 30 years ago – as signaled by Varela, Thompson, and Rosch's 1991 book *The Embodied Mind*, and Rodney Brooks' seminal work on robotics – the cognitive sciences have taken on the notion of embodiment as a central concept: To explain human behavior and cognition, we should not only look at neural processes but also to the body and its interactions with the environment. Given such a general commitment to embodiment, it is important to specify what this commitment entails. The notion of embodied agents is central here.

Embodied Agents

Within the cognitive sciences, embodiment is tied to agents, which in turn are characterized as entities having knowledge and goals in relation to a situation or world in which they can act. The general structure of agent-based explanations incorporates four central ideas. First, such explanations differentiate between a world and an agent that interacts with this world. Second, we have some description of this world, providing us with an *ontology*. Third, we can reuse this ontology to describe the agent itself in terms of intentional or goal-oriented states that incorporate these descriptions, such as in propositional attitudes. Fourth, we assume the agent applies some degree of rational choice with respect to these intentional states and by doing the same, we can predict the actions of the agent. The resulting explanations take familiar forms, such as "When the woman sees the red light, she will stop her car" and "He said he would make lasagna so he must have gone to the supermarket." This basic explanatory structure applies to both simple agents with a basic goal structure as well as complex ones with mental states like beliefs and desires.

In such an account, being an agent is central, while embodiment is an additional constraint. Embodiment is tied to an agent rather than being a substantial entity in its own right. Bodies are important because they instantiate an agent, not the other way round. After all, the standard phrase is "embodied agents," not "agentive bodies." Agents can be conceived and constituted in many different ways, and embodiment can refer to a human body, a simple robot, or even to the interface of a software agent in a simulated environment. There are no evident material criteria involved except for functional requirements that make the entity an agent.

Without clear material criteria, establishing whether some entity is an agent remains a matter of interpretation and ascription. Daniel Dennett's famous notion of an *intentional stance* provides a very influential example of how agent-based explanations work. However, using such an intentional stance and ascribing agency to an entity does not merely come naturally to us. It is actually difficult to avoid and therefore can be thought of as an *intentional urge* rather than an optional theoretical position that we might or might not apply.

Simple movements often suffice to ascribe agency. Humans get upset when they see a robotic device being kicked, and overall humans have a "tendency to innately, automatically, and spontaneously view a broad variety of different targets as holding goals and mental states" (pp. 117–118) as Mar and Macrae phrased it in their 2007 paper *Triggering the Intentional Stance*. One can give evolutionary reasons for the ease with which we discern agents, as agents – predators, group members – which tend to be highly significant and should not remain undetected. Susan Carey, in her 2009 book *The Origin of Concepts,* names agency as one of the "core cognitions" that constitute innate input analyzers that also "ground the deepest ontological commitments and the most general explanatory principles in terms of which we understand our world" (p. 22). Finally, child psychologists Gergely and Csibra, who study the evolutionary and ontogenetic origins of how we interpret others' actions in terms of intentional mental states, report that infants of only 12 months (a) can already interpret others' actions as goal-directed; (b) can evaluate which one of the alternative actions available within the constraints of the situation is the most efficient means to the goal; and (c) expect the agent to perform by the most efficient means available. Taking this all in, ascribing agency is fundamental to our way of looking at the world itself.

Given our tendency to ascribe agency so easily and widely, embodied agents can take many different forms. Embodiment itself need not be specific as long as it provides a material contraption that enables the agent to function. From this perspective, we can – or even should – resist tying human agency too closely to the living human body as this could lead to a form of *biochauvinism* that excludes the possibility of non-biological agents, such as robots. While our bodies enable us to act as agents, these bodies themselves are only relevant for understanding mind and cognition as far as they subserve this agency. Under this interpretation, the many details of our bodies – such as the presence of livers and muscles – are not considered important for the cognitive sciences. Even the relevance of the biological characteristics of the brain can be questioned, as exemplified by science fiction scenarios where minds can be uploaded to a computer leaving the brain behind. Thus, accepting the importance of embodiment, but interpreting this in terms of embodied agency, keeps out the living human body itself as a starting point for the cognitive sciences.

Ascribing agency and intentionality is a basic feature of human minds and comes with a cluster of ideas concerning the limited relevance of our living bodies. However, given our susceptibility to the intentional urge and the intuitive force of the conceptualizations that stem from it, we must consider the possibility that the very salience of agentive interpretations keeps the potentially much wider cognitive relevance of living bodies in the background.

Living Bodies

One reason to be wary about the impact of our intentional urge comes from the rapidly expanding study of cognitively relevant phenomena in a very broad range of living systems. This expanded scope starts with bacteria, but also involves plants, fungi, and both invertebrate and vertebrate animals. Excluding a few exceptions such as humans, these organisms do not have minds nor do they constitute smart agents in any obvious way. Using our intentional urge, this easily disqualifies these cases as interesting targets for the cognitive sciences. However, when studied in more detail, all organisms exhibit behavioral and growth-related decision-making and fit cognitive criteria such as perception, action, memory, and valuing (see Lyon, 2015, for bacteria and Baluška & Levin, 2016, for the general case). Whether we should use the word "cognition" for this broad set of widely dispersed phenomena is a matter of debate, but it is evident that these atypical cases are highly relevant for the cognitive sciences as an explanatory target. In this context, the concept of "agent" becomes less important as a guideline for judging cognitive relevance. Being a living system provides a more certain criterion when these atypical cases are taken into account.

The need to look at living systems more widely provides further reasons for taking our own living bodies seriously as an important target for the cognitive sciences, and even as an empirical condition for agency in the first place. Basic life forms consist of single cells, and are wonders of natural nanotechnology, which enables unicellulars to construct themselves, metabolize, multiply, adapt, change shape, and do all the things that enable them to thrive. Importantly, unicellulars are small. They are usually not visible to the naked eye and live in microscopic worlds. As our own ancestors started out as such unicellulars, it follows that our current perceptual access to a macroscopic world is not a basic situation but the result of major evolutionary changes that took place when our ancestors became multicellular animals.

Becoming multicellular was a major change where (eventually) billions of separate cells came to sense and act as a macroscopic individual. These cells need to be coordinated in many ways, such as for body organization, physiology, and behavior. The evolution of nervous systems must have played a major role in the transition towards multicellular organizations capable of sensing and acting as a collective and, in this way, for the first time becoming capable of accessing our own familiar macroscopic world – the world of extended surfaces and things in it as James Gibson nicely described it in his 1979 book *The Ecological Approach to Visual Perception*. How this transition took place and how it bears on our understanding of nervous systems are key questions for the cognitive sciences, as they turn on explaining how animals turned into the agents that we are so familiar with.

One intriguing idea is that nervous systems originally were mostly involved in controlling the body itself, enabling it to move in a co-ordinated way. The resulting motile body could then have acted as a multicellular unit capable of sensing in a way that was dispersed across many cells and so enabling perceptual access of the macro-scopic world (see Keijzer, 2015, for more details and references). If this is on the right track, it ties the ontology of the perceptual and behavioral world to the makeup of a living body. How we should interpret this option remains future work, but we will need to reas-sess many assumptions that seem clear and fundamental from our own human perspective, which is itself tied to such a multicellular organization.

Our living animal bodies incorporate many characteristics that may be crucial for understanding our minds and cognition. The concept of "agent" provides a skewed perspective on our own living bodies that backgrounds much that is relevant. Using the concept of (embodied) agents as a starting point for the cognitive sciences ignores not only a wide array of fundamental questions about the origins and nature of such agents, but also keeps these questions invisible by downplaying the crucial role of the living body.

Lived Bodies

One final issue must be addressed. Within *phenomenology* and *en-activism* (two related philosophical approaches that both focus on conscious experience), the concept of a living body is often used as a contrast to the *lived body* (see, for example, Evan Thompson's 2007 book, *Mind in Life*). The lived body refers here to our first-person experience of our own bodies and aims to describe it from this perspective. Advocates for this perspective argue that study of the living body is limited to a third-person scientific perspective on the body that is associated with a reductive view that neglects experience.

There are various reasons for being unhappy with this restricted view of the living body that sees it as disconnected from first-person experience, which only surfaces in the "lived body." Foremost, highlighting the experiential lived body brings us back to high-level agentive conceptualizations of the body that fit in with an agentive interpretation. Such a view easily remains oblivious to the under-lying complexity and organization of our own bodies that can only be accessed by systematic, empirical, and socially shared scientific work. Another reason concerns the critique that scientific work on the living body involves a reductive view that is antithetical to conscious experience. Although such a reductive tendency has indeed been present in a lot of scientific work, by now the need to explain consciousness as we all experience it firsthand has become part of the scientific enterprise (see Ginsburg & Jablonka, 2019, for an overview). When the cognitive sciences start to pay attention to the living body in earnest, this inquiry must also involve the question of how a first-person perspective and the experience associated with it comes into being in the natural world. We do not need a dualism between living and lived bodies.

For Sources and Further Reading

Baluška, F., & Levin, M. (2016). On having no head: Cognition throughout biological systems. *Frontiers in Psychology, 7,* 902.

Csibra, G., & Gergely, G. (2013). Teleological understanding of actions. In M. R. Banaji & S. A. Gelman (Eds.), *Navigating the social world: What infants, children, and other species can teach us* (pp. 38–43). New York: Oxford University Press.

Ginsburg, S., & Jablonka, E. (2019). *The evolution of the sensitive soul: Learning and the origins of consciousness.* Cambridge: MIT Press.

Keijzer, F. A. (2015). Moving and sensing without input and output: Early nervous systems and the origins of the animal sensorimotor organization. *Biology & Philosophy, 30*(3), 311–331.

Lyon, P. (2015). The cognitive cell: Bacterial behavior reconsidered. *Frontiers in Microbiology, 6,* 264.

7 Approaching Learning Hands First

How Gesture Influences Thought

Susan Goldin-Meadow

The gestures that speakers spontaneously produce as they talk are acts of the body and, as such, have the potential to influence learning in the same way that bodily action does. But gesture differs from action in a number of important respects and, as a result, helps learners remember newly learned information and extend that information to new contexts better than action does.

When people talk, they move their hands. These hand movements, commonly called *gestures,* can convey substantive information that is related, but not always identical, to the information conveyed in that talk. Take, for example, a child telling a room full of adults that she ran upstairs. She says, *I runned up*, while at the same time moving her hand in an upward spiral. We know from her hands, and only from her hands, that she ran up a spiral staircase. Gesture thus has the potential to offer listeners – parents, teachers, clinicians, researchers – insight into a speaker's unspoken thoughts.

In fact, when a speaker's gesture about a task conveys different information from that speaker's speech, it signals that the speaker is open to instruction on that task. For example, a child who says she solved the mathematical equivalence problem, 2+5+3=__+3, by adding up the numbers to the left of the equals sign ("I added 2 plus 5 plus 3") while, at the same time, gesturing to all of the numbers in the problem (point at the 2, the 5, the 3 on the left, and the 3 on the right), is more likely to profit from a math lesson on the problem than a child whose gestures match her speech (point at the 2, the 5, and the 3 on the left). The gestures that a learner produces can thus reveal that the learner is in a transitional state and, in this sense, ready to learn.

But gesture can do more than reveal a speaker's thoughts – it can change those thoughts and, as a result, contribute to learning. More specifically, the gestures that learners see can help them learn, as can the gestures that learners produce. For example, children are more likely to learn how to solve a mathematical equivalence problem if their teachers gesture during the lesson than if they don't gesture. Children are also more likely to learn how to solve the problems if they are taught gestures that they themselves produce during the math lesson than if they are not taught gestures and are taught only words to say during the lesson.

Why does gesture have an impact on learning? One possibility is that gesture is part of a multi-modal production involving both hand (gesture) and mouth (speech). If this hypothesis is correct, then signers who use the same modality (the manual modality) to both sign and gesture should *not* show these learning effects. But they do – signers whose gestures convey different information from their signs prior to instruction in mathematical equivalence are more likely to learn how to solve the math problems than signers whose gestures convey the same information as their signs. And signers whose math teachers gesture along with their signs benefit from that instruction, just as speakers do when their teachers gesture along with their speech. It is not the juxtaposition of hand and mouth that gives gesture its power – it's more likely to be the gesture's ability to provide an analog representational format that co-occurs, and is coordinated, with the discrete representational format found in language, be it speech or sign.

Another possibility is that gestures are movements of the hand and, as such, actions of the body – in other words, gesture may affect learning because it is itself an action. Actions have indeed been found to affect cognition. For example, people are more likely to recall an action if they have done the action than if they have read a verbal description of the action. And learners are more likely to master a task if they produce an action relevant to the task than if they see others produce the action. Not surprisingly, when a task is learned by doing an action, motor areas in the brain are activated. What is more surprising is that these same motor areas are activated later when the task is done *without* action. This same process happens when a task is learned through gesture: Motor areas are activated after the task has been learned when it is performed without gesture. Acting while learning a task – be it acting on an object or gesturing in the air – thus has long-term effects on how the task is processed, even when the actions are no longer involved in doing the task.

But gesture differs from action in a number of important respects. First, gestures *refer* to the world and thus do not directly influence it. For example, producing a *hammer* gesture does not actually flatten the object – only physically hammering the object has this effect. Second, although gestures, particularly iconic gestures (i.e., gestures that look like what they represent), resemble actions, gestures vary in how closely they mirror the actions they represent. For example, a *hammer* gesture produced with a C-shaped hand simulating how the hammer would be held if it were moved up and down resembles the actual act of hammering more closely than a *hammer* gesture produced with a pointing hand. Gesture can therefore selectively highlight components of action that are relevant to a particular situation. This selectivity could allow gesture to play a different role in learning than action does.

As it turns out, gesture and action do play different roles, not in learning *per se*, but in retaining the knowledge gained and in extending that knowledge to new contexts. For example, when children are taught a novel word (e.g., *leeming*) along with either an action (e.g., squeezing the bulb of an object) or a gesture representing that action (e.g., squeezing performed near but not on the object), they are equally good at learning the new word. However, children who learned through gesture are more likely to generalize the new word to appropriate contexts (i.e., to other objects that have the potential to be *leemed*) than children who learned through action – and this difference widens over time.

As another example, consider a child who is either taught to solve mathematical equivalence problems by gesturing the grouping strategy (e.g., for the problem, $2+5+3=\_\_+3$, pointing with a V-hand at the 2 and the 5, the two numbers that should be grouped and summed, and then pointing at the blank), or by acting out the grouping strategy on plastic numbers that have been placed on the problem (e.g., picking up the 2 and the 5, and holding the two numbers together in the blank). Children are equally good at learning how to solve the mathematical equivalence problem whether they are taught through gesture or through action. But children who learned through gesture are more likely to generalize the knowledge they gained to new problem formats (e.g., $2+5+3=2+\_\_$, or $2+5+3=\_\_+4$) than children who learned through action. Both gesture and action help learners learn, but gesture helps them extend and retain that learning, two essential components of education.

These facts about gesture have implications for practice, in particular, for how gesture can be recruited in everyday teaching situations by parents and teachers. A good teaching tool is one that can be implemented broadly. If a tool is difficult to use, it is unlikely to be adopted. If the tool is costly, it may not be accessible to underprivileged communities. Gesture is an ideal teaching tool because it is ubiquitous, naturally produced, and universally accessible in both homes and schools. Moreover, gesture is not only used naturally, but its use can be increased in children, parents, and teachers with little effort. Adults can be told to use gestures when talking to children and will thus model gestures for them. They can also be told to ask children to produce gestures of their own. These practices have the potential to be particularly beneficial for children from lower socio-economic homes who tend to produce fewer spontaneous gestures than children from higher socio-economic homes. In addition, because children who have impairments in language often use gesture to compensate for their disabilities, harnessing gesture may be beneficial not only for typically developing children but also for children with special needs.

There are, however, at least two caveats to consider. First, gesture is a powerful tool that can be used to promote learning, but it can also be used to mislead. For example, a math teacher inadvertently pointed at all four numbers, without pausing at the equals sign, in the problem 2+5+3=__+3. In response, her pupil added up the numbers and gave 13 as his (incorrect) answer – he was misled by his teacher's gestures. As another example from eyewitness testimony, interviewers are told to ask open-ended questions (e.g., "What else was he wearing?"), rather than targeted questions (e.g., "What color was the hat he was wearing?"), to avoid influencing their witnesses. But an open-ended question produced along with a suggestive gesture (e.g., a donning-hat movement) results in as many incorrect responses (in this case, that he was wearing a hat even though he wasn't) as a targeted question produced without gesture. Gesture is a powerful tool that needs to be used thoughtfully.

Second, gesture may not always be *the* optimal tool. Although gesture often leads to more flexible learning than actions on objects, there may be times when action experience is more effective than gesture. For example, a child who has made very little progress in mastering a task may profit more from action than from gesture simply because acting on an object can provide a concrete, physical representation of a concept. Manipulatives are often used in math classrooms for this purpose. However, the danger in using action manipulatives exclusively is that learners may not be able to generalize what they have learned to new contexts. Offering learners gesture *after* they have used manipulatives to make progress on a task may, for some tasks and for some learners, be just the right teaching strategy to promote deep and lasting learning.

The facts about gesture described here also have theoretical implications for notions of embodiment. Gesture's impact on the learning process cannot stem exclusively from the fact that it involves the body – actions on objects are embodied, too, and they do not encourage learners to generalize in the way that gesture does. The body may be important for gesture to have an impact on learning not because it is embodied *per se*, but because it offers an analog format within which to represent ideas that are different from those supported by speech. Gesture thus promotes a second representational format that has the potential to lead to learning.

To summarize, gesture offers a unique window onto a speaker's thoughts, and provides a vehicle not only for changing those thoughts but also for promoting deep and lasting learning. Importantly, gesture can improve learning with little effort or cost. Simply telling children to gesture, or modeling gesture for them, puts gesture into the hands of the learners. And increasing child gesture improves learning by giving parents and teachers insight into a child's cutting-edge (albeit implicit) thoughts, and by helping the child consolidate those thoughts and make them more explicit. Along the same lines, simply telling parents and teachers to gesture, or modeling gesture for them, puts gesture into the hands of the teachers. And increasing teacher gesture not only increases child gesture, but also encourages teachers to express imagistic ideas that may be easier to grasp in the manual modality than in the oral modality. Gesture is a ubiquitous and easily accessible tool that should be harnessed for teaching and learning.

For Sources and Further Reading

Cartmill, E. A., Beilock, S., & Goldin-Meadow, S. (2012). A word in the hand: Action, gesture, and mental representation in humans and non-human primates. *Philosophical Transactions of the Royal Society, Series B, 367*, 129–143.

Goldin-Meadow, S. (2014). How gesture works to change our minds. *Trends in Neuroscience and Education (TiNE), 3*, 4–6.

Goldin-Meadow, S. (2015). From action to abstraction: Gesture as a mechanism of change. *Developmental Review, 38*, 167–184.

Goldin-Meadow, S., & Alibali, M. W. (2013). Gesture's role in speaking, learning, and creating language. *Annual Review of Psychology, 64*, 257–283.

Novack, M., & Goldin-Meadow, S. (2017). Gesture as representational action: A paper about function. *Psychonomic Bulletin and Review, 24*(3), 652–665.

8 Digitization, Reading, and the Body

Handling Texts on Paper and Screens

Anne Mangen

The ongoing transition from paper/print to screens reveals the extent to which reading is multisensory and embodied, involving in particular our fingers and hands in manually engaging with a text.

Our modes of reading are changing. Whether we are reading to pass time on our way to work, are studying for an exam in the library, or are browsing through today's news or enjoying a novel at home – in many of these cases, reading entails engaging with a digital screen device rather than with materials printed on the substrate of paper. Laptops, tablets, and smart phones are doing the job of "old" reading technologies such as print books and newspapers, while also being multipurpose devices with which we entertain ourselves with movies, chat with friends and family, pay our bills, and coordinate our children's school activities.

Digitization is massively and rapidly affecting our reading behavior, and it is futile to try to give a simple, general answer to the question of whether we read "better" or "worse" as an effect of this transition. Such questions require fine-tuning in terms of what type of text/material we have in mind (narrative texts or news entries? Long or short texts? Simple or complex?), the purpose of reading (study? Leisure? Information updates?), the type of device (desktop computer? Smart phone?), the physical location (at the office? On the train or at a cabin)? Indeed, Anežka Kuzmičová and her colleagues (see Kuzmičová et al., 2018) have shown that physical location and social context – whether a reader is, for instance, alone or in the company of others – may affect aspects of reading, such as supporting the sense of immersion or the conjuring of mental imagery. Other factors probably matter, too. Amidst all these changes, one dimension emerges as being more fundamental than hitherto acknowledged: the role of the body, and of embodiment, in reading.

Whether for study, pleasure, or information, we typically read by holding the text in our hands. Reading has always been embodied, inviting and requiring certain postures and dexterous movements to access and process the texts. The ongoing replacement of print books with digital devices brings the *haptics* of reading to the fore, inviting us to reconsider the role of embodiment for cognitive as well as emotional aspects. Often called "active touch," haptics is an umbrella term for the combination of senses of touch via the skin, and movement of our joints and limbs – most typically, our fingers and hands. Applied to reading, haptics refers to the ways in which we use our fingers and hands to hold the text and the device on which the text is displayed, the ways we turn the pages back and forth, use our index finger to guide and sharpen our visual gaze, and use our fingers as place holders. For a long time, thanks to the dominance of the print book, the embodied aspects of reading have not been granted much attention. However, with much of our reading now performed with a screen device rather than with paper, the embodiment – in particular, the haptics – of reading takes on fresh urgency.

Take a closer look at your fingers next time you pick up your smart phone to check the news, and compare with your fingers as they handle the pages of a print magazine. Or, take a moment during your reading of a novel on the Kindle or iPad, to reflect on the feel when holding the device and swiping the screen to turn the pages. Then compare this with page-turning in a print book. The materiality of the *substrate* – screen displays and paper pages – provides different tactile feedback to your fingers and hands, hence engaging your body and brain differently. Whether, how and to what extent such differences have an effect on how we read, are intriguing questions that reading researchers are only beginning to understand, and findings from empirical research on screen reading indicate that there is indeed more to reading than meets the eye. More specifically, the physicality of the substrate of paper may contribute to certain cognitive and emotional aspects of reading in ways that we have yet to fully acknowledge and comprehend.

A wealth of research has compared paper and screen reading, from reading fairytales in print and on tablets with toddlers and preschoolers, to studies measuring recall and comprehension among high school students reading print text books and their digital equivalents, to adults reading novels in book format and on tablets and e-readers. The diversity of methodologies, designs, and texts used, precludes a simple answer to the question of "P(rint) vs E(lectronic)." However, recent meta-analyses (see Delgado et al., 2018, as an example) have shown that, for the reading of informational texts, there is a *screen inferiority* when it comes to reading comprehension. In other words, people tend to comprehend a text better when they read it on paper compared to reading it on a screen. Moreover, the difference in reading comprehension in favor of paper has in fact *increased* rather than decreased over the past couple of decades. Such findings cast serious doubts on persistent claims about digital natives being better at reading on screens than on paper.

The reasons provided for the screen inferiority are related to what is called "The Shallowing Hypothesis" (see Wolf, 2018). Given that our most common modes of engaging with texts occur online, we acquire a habit of quickly perusing an enormous amount of text and information, rarely stopping to engage with any of it more deeply and conscientiously. These screen-based habits then "bleed over," to use Wolf's term, to our mode of reading on paper – resulting in the feeling that our concentration starts to drift after a couple of pages, and that we have to make an effort to stay focused. As Nicholas Carr observed in *The Atlantic* in 2008, "The deep reading that used to come naturally has become a struggle."

Why do many of us find it so difficult to engage in deep reading and, concomitantly, deep thinking, on screen? Plausible explanations can be found in the embodied dimensions of reading and in the differences in *sensorimotor contingencies* between screens and paper as substrates for text presentation. Sensorimotor contingencies refer to the sets of structured laws prescribing the sensory changes brought about by one's movement and/or manipulation of objects: How we perceive the look, smell, sound and feel of objects in our surroundings depends on how we move around in the world, and manipulate and move objects around in, most often, our hands.

These laws are specific to the various sense modalities, meaning that the sensorimotor contingencies for vision are different from those for hearing, which are yet again different from those of the sense of touch, smell, etc. Moving an object around in our hands will provide abundant information about its properties – texture, size, shape, weight, etc., only some of which are available when we merely look at the object. However, when seeing an apple on the kitchen counter, our numerous prior, embodied experiences with simultaneously seeing and touching an apple will shape our predictions about what it will feel like if/when we pick it up and move it around in our hand. Vision and touch are intimately entwined in our ongoing perception and experience of our surroundings – vision, and therefore also reading, is "textured." This texture is provided by the substrate on which the text is displayed – whether sheets of paper bound together in a book, a piece of cardboard, or an LCD touch screen.

Importantly, the sensorimotor contingencies of the book differ from those of a screen: A text may look identical when printed on a page and displayed on a tablet screen, but the two texts differ with respect to the kinesthetic feedback they provide. When we read a print book, we can see as well as feel the page-by-page progress through the text. The physicality of paper allows a sense of volume to the substrate, which embodies – literally speaking – the text and reflects its length. Hence, just by a look at the spine, you can immediately see – and feel – whether a book on the shelf is an 800-page long novel, or a 20-page short story. In contrast, when you read on a screen, there is no such correspondence between the physicality of the substrate (screen) and the length and extension of the text embedded therein. We can *see*, by means of progress bars or other visual indicators (e.g., page numbers), where in the text we are. However, differently from with a book, this exclusively visual feedback is not supported by the associated sensorimotor cues.

This *intangibility* of the digital text may have implications for cognitive and emotional aspects of reading. For instance, several studies find that people – younger as well as older – still prefer paper over screens, especially when reading longer texts (e.g. Mizrachi et al., 2018). The reasons given for the preference for paper often have to do with tangibility and the tactile quality: People report that the feel of paper helps them focus and concentrate, and that something is missing when they read on a screen. This phenomenon, which Gerlach and Buxmann (2011) called "haptic dissonance," is found even with younger readers – the so-called "digital natives" for whom screen reading is the new normal.

Moreover, recent research indicates that the missing sensorimotor – kinesthetic – feedback of screens may in fact negatively affect certain cognitive aspects of reading. In a 2019 experiment, my colleagues and I compared the reading of a long (28-page) plot-based story read on a Kindle and on paper in a print pocket book. Matching the surface dimensions of the paper pages to the Kindle display so that the texts *looked* identical, page-by-page, we assessed participants' performance on a range of measures targeting factual recall and comprehension. Participants performed equally well on most of the tasks; however, on measures related to their ability to correctly reconstruct the temporality and order of events, those who had read the text in a print pocket book outperformed the Kindle group.

We should of course be cautious when interpreting findings from one single experiment, so replications are needed before we can conclude on this issue. However, it seems justified to claim that the tangibility and kinaesthetic feedback of paper seems to play a role in cognitive – and perhaps even emotional – processes, in part explaining the observed screen inferiority for certain aspects of reading.

"Smell and sight are relevant senses when it comes to reading. But touch may well be the most important," writes Naomi Baron (2015, p. 142). Hence, future research on reading would do well to broaden the lens, accommodating the vital contributions of our hands, fingers, and embodied minds in the reading process.

For Sources and Further Reading

Baron, N. (2015). *Words onscreen: The fate of reading in a digital world.* New York: Oxford University Press.

Delgado, P., Vargas, C., Ackerman, R., and Salmerón, L. (2018). Don't throw away your printed books: A meta-analysis on the effects of reading media on comprehension. *Educational Research Review, 25,* 23–38.

Gerlach, J., & Buxmann, P. (2011). Investigating the acceptance of electronic books: The impact of haptic dissonance on innovation adoption. *European Conference on Information Systems (ECIS) Proceedings,* 141.

Kuzmičová, A., Dias, P., Čepič, A. V., Albrechtslund A. B., Casado, A., Topić, M. K., ... Teixeira-Botelho, I. (2018). Reading and company: Embodiment and social space in silent reading practices. *Literacy, 52*(2), 70–77.

Mangen, A., Olivier, G., & Velay, J. L. (2019). Comparing comprehension of a long text read in print book and on Kindle: Where in the text and when in the story? *Frontiers in Psychology, 10,* 38.

Mizrachi, D., Salaz, A. M., Kurbanoglu, S., Boustany, J., & ARFIS Research Group (2018). Academic reading format preferences and behaviors among university students worldwide: A comparative survey analysis. *PloS one, 13*(5), e0197444.

Wolf, M. (2018). *Reader, come home: The reading brain in a digital world.* New York: Harper.

Part III

Coordinating

What call-and-response relationships attune the body to the world around it and orchestrate its inner workings? Through what sorts of clocks, recursive loops, and other controls are physiology and action coordinated with environmental rhythms, emotion, and thinking? The essays in this section take up these questions, describing how bodies oscillate in tribute to rhythms of the distant past and adjust in real time to circumstances and goals.

9 Embodied Time
A Shared, Ancient Heritage

Barbara Helm

On our deeply rhythmic planet, life has evolved the ability to embody the change between day and night, the seasons, tides, and
phases of the moon. Human societies strive to overcome this rhythmicity by generating ever-ready "24/7" conditions, but problems
linked to clock disruption remind us that we are better off accepting, and staying tuned with, our rhythmically changing bodies.

The fundamental condition of our planet is deep rhythmicity (see
Figure 9.1): Earth's annual orbit around sun marks the seasons; rotation around Earth's axis causes the alternation between day and
night; moon's monthly orbit around Earth is perceived as periodic
waxing and waning; and lunar gravitational forces generate the
tides on the rotating Earth. These rhythms, and resulting physical
changes – for example, in light, temperature, and ocean currents –
shape the cycles of living organisms. Striking rhythmic processes
are the annual die-back and regeneration of green vegetation, the
migrations of billions of animals, and the well-timed dawn chorus
of birds and evening emergence of bats.

Such easily observable biotic mass phenomena result from individual *biological* rhythms of a myriad of organisms. They are the
most obvious tip of an iceberg of countless rhythms in body function, from expression of genes and cell regeneration, through fluc-
tuations of body temperature and hormones, to cycles in abilities,
such as physical strength and the ability to concentrate. Biological
rhythms are maintained by organisms ranging from unicells (such
as dinoflagellates, zooplankton, beer yeast) to flowers, bees, birds,
and mammals.

Importantly, these rhythms are *endogenous* (i.e., self-generated).
Each individual organism carries inside itself a biological clock
that continues to tick, even if the individual is isolated from all

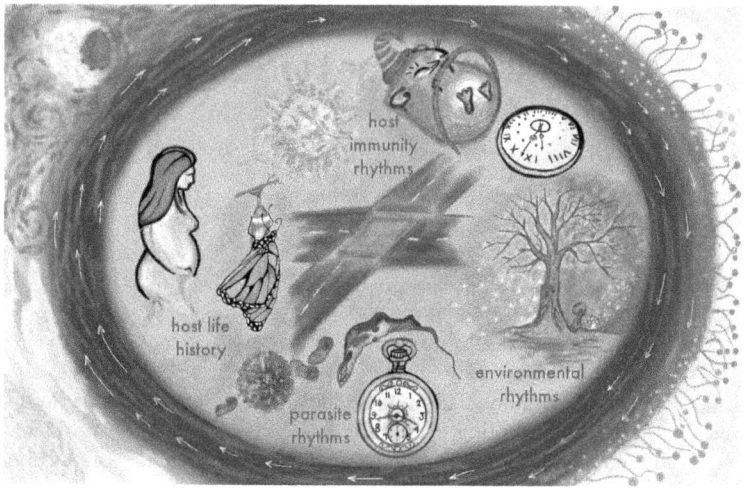

Figure 9.1 Rhythms of humans and other organisms are caused by planetary movements of Earth (circular image) and moon relative to sun. In anticipation of annual, daily, lunar, and tidal cycles, organisms from all biological kingdoms have evolved internal time-keeping. Examples include timely hibernation, pregnancy, and eclosion of butterflies. That these rhythms of organisms are entwined is illustrated for host and parasite interactions. Host and parasite are both subject to environmental rhythms. Hosts may ramp up immune defense at anticipated time of parasite attack, whereas a parasite may attempt to circumvent or manipulate the host's rhythmic immune defense. Figure is reprinted in grayscale from a color version created by Micaela Martinez-Bakker that appeared in Martinez-Bakker & Helm (2015), *Trends in Ecology & Evolution.*

environmental information. This phenomenon was first described in the 18th century for plants that, despite being stored away from light, continued to show daily movements of their leaves. Since then, studies of countless organisms have confirmed that their cycles – for example, in activity and rest or in hibernation and reproduction – continued under entirely constant conditions. Humans are no exception, as firmly established by the rhythmicity of scores of volunteers who have allowed themselves to be studied for days or weeks in caves or custom-built isolation facilities without access to the external environment. It also is true that biological rhythms have evolved to interact with the environment of organisms. Under natural conditions, the rhythms do entrain to reliable signals in the

environment, most commonly to the rhythmic changes in light conditions arising from planetary movement. But the cycles carry on
even in the absence of environmental signals, a still-vital legacy of
rhythms in the distant past.

The best-known biological rhythms are *circadian* (i.e., endogenous
rhythms that repeat at an approximately daily time scale). Research
has tracked the mechanism of these rhythms in many species to a set
of genes that interact in a feedback loop, to effectively switch each
other on and off through the proteins they encode. In this way, a simple cell – for example, in human skin or in the brain – can generate its
own rhythm. Its apparently simple loop is backed up and fine-tuned
by a whole suite of additional genes, more feedback loops, modifi-
ers and epigenetic changes. Moreover, the many cells of individual
organisms – billions in the case of the human brain alone – need to
be coordinated in their rhythmicity. Elaborate mechanisms enable
communication and synchronization of the many clocks in the body
to yield an overall representation of "time."

The sophistication and ubiquity of biological clocks suggest that
over evolutionary time, organisms have greatly benefitted from
embodying time. Planetary rhythms have been entirely reliable
throughout most of the evolution of life, and certainly throughout
human history. Consequently, organisms had ample time to tune
their bodies to the rhythmic changes in their environments. A number of advantages are associated with embodied time. First, body
functions are activated for the time when they are needed. For example, body temperature is high at times of physical activity, and
immune capacities such as wound healing are high when injury or
infections are most likely. Complementarily, body functions can be
down-regulated at other times to allow for regeneration and rest,
so that different processes are active at different times. Secondly,
embodied time allows coordination of such different processes in
the body so that, for example, competing activities do not co-occur.
Thirdly, embodied time allows for the correct interpretation of the
natural environment. For example, bees and birds are able to nav-
igate by the position of the sun, accounting for its apparent movement across the sky. Finally, embodied time allows organisms to
anticipate relevant changes in the environment long before they occur. For example, pregnancy and egg-laying occur well in advance
of the favorable environmental conditions in which newly born
young can thrive.

Humans currently have an ambiguous relationship with biological rhythms. On the one hand, rhythmicity has long been keenly

observed. Ancient knowledge, put in stone as a Mayan pyramid or Stonehenge circle, reflected minute awareness of planetary cycles. Many cultures also observed nature's cycles, such as birds' daily morning chorus or annual migrations, with similar acuity. Knowledge of the planet's rhythms had imminent relevance for agriculture, hunting, or travel by land and sea, and that knowledge came to be canonized in a wide range of calendars and clocks. Many cultures had also recognized rhythmic changes in the human body, such as in temperament and in reproductive rhythms associated with lunar and annual calendars. On the other hand, an alternative conceptualization of time as linear and disembodied came to be important for humans. This view increasingly dominated physics to history, religion, and performing arts. This trend resulted in a baffling paucity of language, with the word "time" being used to refer to radically different concepts. Moreover, as modern fascination with "progress" grew, the linear view of time came to overshadow, if not discredit, the view of time as rhythmic, shared, and embodied. A richer understanding of time is warranted. Although linear progress of time can have bodily traces – for example, as tempo in performance or in processes of development and aging – it is the rhythmic nature of time whose embodiment is shared from humans to unicells.

With increasing human power over the immediate rhythmic environment – light and darkness, heat and cold – rhythmic bodily time fell into disfavor. Many modern cultures came to consider human lives as a-seasonal, derided lunar rhythms as mythology, and strove to overcome daily rhythms. We are currently well on our way towards a "24/7" life-style (i.e., continuous activity around the clock throughout the week), where around the year humans expose themselves to the daylength and temperature of eternal summer. The proportion of workers doing night shifts continues to increase, reaching approximately 15% in several industrialized countries. Worryingly, human changes affect rhythmic environments of all organisms on a global scale. The darkness of night, which has been key for entrainment of biological clocks, is lost at a frightening rate. Meanwhile, global warming modifies the seasons and along with it, disconnects the finely timed network of organisms' interactions, for example in food webs, pollination, and host-parasite systems.

Ironically, efforts of abandoning rhythmicity in human societies coincided with increasingly acute and painful awareness of the shared, ancient heritage of embodied time. The persistence of our circadian rhythm is experienced through jet-lag – that is, a mismatch between body-time and environmental time after flying across time zones. Clearly, resetting the watch does not suffice to shift ourselves to new locations. Instead, well-timed light exposure, strict sleep regimens, pharmaceutical solutions, or simply patience is required to overcome the restless nights and fatigued days of a mismatched clock. Other forms of clock disruption that are less immediate than jet-lag pose still greater risks to humans. Shift-work has been identified as a major cause of a broad range of human pathologies and is associated with heightened risk of errors and accidents. Additionally, mental health issues are often associated with disturbed clocks, and sleep disorders and sleep deprivation affect many societies at epidemiological scales.

Such observations have prompted the insight that we humans, once again, act as a naively arrogant species in any attempt to deny our embodiment of planetary rhythms. Human rhythmicity is now well-documented on daily, lunar, and annual time-scales. Although these findings might slow some ambitions, there is so much to be gained from humble acceptance of embodied time. For example, we now know that individual differences between so-called "owls and larks" (i.e., evening and morning chronotypes) have a firm physiological basis. Chronotype also changes dramatically with age, in particular during puberty. No longer can evening types be stereotyped as lazy, nor morning types as boring, once the reality of biological rhythms is acknowledged. *Chrono-medicine* opens new possibilities through, for example, flu vaccinations or medications that are more efficient if applied at a generally appropriate or even a personalized body-time. On the other end of the spectrum, reference to embodied time also defines our relationship with other organisms, towards a cross-disciplinary advancement of *One Health* for humans, other animals, and the global environment.

For Sources and Further Reading

Foster, R. G., & Kreitzman, L. (2005). *Rhythms of life: The biological clocks that control the daily lives of every living thing.* New Haven, CT: Yale University Press.

Foster, R. G., & Kreitzman, L. (2009). *Seasons of life: The biological rhythms that enable living things to thrive and survive.* New Haven, CT: Yale University Press.

Martinez-Bakker, M., & Helm, B. (2015). The influence of biological rhythms on host-parasite interactions. *Trends in Ecology & Evolution, 30*(6), 314–326.

Martinez, M. E. (2018). The calendar of epidemics: Seasonal cycles of infectious diseases. *PLOS Pathogens, 14*(11), e1007327.

Roenneberg, T., & Merrow, M. (2016). The circadian clock and human health. *Current Biology, 26*(10), R432–R443.

Schwartz, W., Helm, B., & Gerkema, M. (Eds.). (2017). *Wild clocks: Integrating chronobiology and ecology to understand timekeeping in free-living animals.* London: Philosophical Transactions of the Royal Society B: Biological Sciences.

Wehr, T. A. (2001). Photoperiodism in humans and other primates: Evidence and implications. *Journal of Biological Rhythms, 16*(4), 348–364.

10 Rhythm and the Body

Gregory A. Bryant

Rhythm involves the production and perception of regularly timed events. It is inextricably tied to body movement and an embodied sense of interpersonal coordination in social and musical contexts that triggers reward centers in our brains, suggesting evolutionary function.

Rhythm is ubiquitous. Many phenomena in nature have rhythmic qualities, occurring on highly variable timescales, and for many different reasons. Natural systems in living organisms are no exception. Our hearts beat in periodic intervals, our breathing functions in regular cycles, and basic body motions such as walking require a complicated rhythmic coordination between interacting motor systems. For living beings, rhythm is embodied, meaning that it emanates from bodily experience, and manifests itself in both body movement patterns and our perceptual sensitivities. Many of us cannot help but move along to a rhythmic sound, especially when it is in the context of music. Recognizing the role of the body in rhythmic phenomena constitutes a crucial turn in our understanding of the importance of rhythm in human experience, as well as the evolution of many human behaviors.

The word "rhythm" is derived from the Greek *rhiem*, meaning "to flow." The notion of flow is a central conceptual basis for recent work in the psychology of rhythm and music, and studies of how musicians "get in the groove." But the idea of flowing rhythmically extends well beyond music: We get in the flow with others in conversation, or with ourselves in our work, and with our lives in the broadest sense. The underlying conceptual metaphor of flowing is rooted in our physical experiences of moving through the world and understanding that movement as a kind of journey. This metaphorical understanding is revealed in how people talk about many aspects of life in these terms, including quite importantly, how it feels to get in the groove, or flow with others. Flowing is intrinsically rewarding, and various kinds of embodied descriptions are indicative of the deep interactions between sensorimotor systems, perceptually guided action, and cognitive structure.

Most generally, rhythm refers to specific kinds of timing phenomena that can be described in terms of relationships between events. Rhythmic events can be *isochronic* (equally timed intervals) or *heterochronic* (variably timed intervals), sometimes with quite complex, hierarchical structures. Although laypeople and scholars alike often use the term rhythmic coordination in somewhat loose ways, the idea of entrainment is actually quite specific (see Phillips-Silver et al., 2010, for a review). Entrainment is the coupling of independent *oscillators* made possible by an energy transfer between them. An oscillator is any system that produces periodic output, such as a pendulum or metronome. Imagine two metronomes rocking back and forth separately, at two different beats per minute (BPM). They will not spontaneously assume the same period, of course, unless they are positioned in a way where their movement can have mutual physical effects on one another. For instance, if they are on a wood board, which is set on a sturdy surface, there will be no way for the motion of the swinging pendulum arms to move the board, and thus affect the other metronome(s). But if they are placed on a board with wheels, allowing it to move along with the motion of the metronomes, the movement of the pendulum arms will shift the board back and forth. This motion creates a means of energy transfer between the two metronomes, resulting in a feedback process that causes the two oscillators to become coupled, with the coupling dependent on the strength of the energetic connection. The independent oscillator settings (in BPM) can disrupt the entrainment, resulting in a continuously shifting phase relationship (itself potentially comprising a higher-order rhythmic structure). A web search of metronome synchronization will result in many visual examples.

Now imagine two bodies as the oscillators, and the link between perception and action as the means of energy transfer. What we hear (and see) can directly affect how we move our bodies; that is, auditory perception is attuned to isochronous sounds, and our bodies naturally engage with those sounds. From an embodiment perspective, we can understand rhythmic production and perception as situated activity that guides recurrent sensorimotor connectivity. Bodies generate rhythms through specialized motor programs, often with the help of culturally evolved technology, and drive perceptually guided action. Even passive listening to musical rhythms will activate motor areas of the brain. In many ways, rhythm processing in any animal provides a quintessential example of the relevance of embodied processes for understanding perception and action.

The link between rhythmic production and perception mediated through embodied processes can function in many social contexts. Social entrainment is present in a variety of species (e.g., synchronous chorusing in crickets and frogs), often in the service of territorial and mating behavior; however, many animals can be trained to entrain, with varying success. Researchers have studied parrots, sea lions, bonobos, and others showing how these animals can move contingently to a rhythmic stimulus. But none of these particular species have been observed to spontaneously engage in social entrainment with one another in nature. One proposed source of entrainment abilities is vocal learning. Being able to produce target vocal sounds generated by others requires specialized perception of useful acoustic features that interfaces with vocal motor machinery – a perception–action link. Put simply, vocal learning often requires that we connect, with precise timing, what we hear to how we move. Evidence from nonhuman animal research shows that spontaneous contingent movement to rhythmic sounds is typically performed by vocal learners, such as parrots. But with extensive training, non-vocal learners do it as well, though the underlying mechanisms are unknown. In one case, a California sea lion (not a vocal learner) has been shown to have learned quite well how to bob his head to the beat of human music. But closely related seal species are vocal learners, suggesting that latent abilities shared across genera or families could be at play. Evolutionary processes conserve structure, and thus, mechanisms can potentially be triggered by certain input despite their absence in the behavioral repertoire of the animal. The vocal learning hypothesis does a fairly good job of explaining why rhythm entrainment exists in many animals who do not show spontaneous social entrainment, but more work is needed (see Ravignani et al., 2014, for a review).

Rhythm in humans has been described as a suite of co-operating behavioral subskills, including *continuous* and *burst* body muscle movement (sometimes called *smooth* and *ballistic*), the action-perception link just described, and error correction mechanisms. Specific types of errors require tailored behavioral solutions. For example, adjusting your rhythmic behavior timing to synchronize with a beat that is the same tempo as your movement (e.g., stop momentarily and start on time) is a different problem from adjusting the interval between rhythmic events (i.e., change the BPM). Evidence suggests these kinds of corrections involve distinct cortical processes. The underlying control and implementation of error correction mechanisms interface in still unknown ways with subjective feelings of being in the groove. This sensorimotor coordination is facilitated by many factors, including the auditory structure of the rhythm, whether the target beat is generated by a live agent or a machine, and how easily one can imagine and produce entrained movement.

Consider the qualities of music and the contexts in which people are compelled to dance. We have to *feel* the beat and find a way to move our bodies contingently. For instance, people tend to move their upper body, especially their head, to salient low frequency features in rhythms (e.g., a kick drum), while moving their torso and hands to more high-frequency components. But simple isochrony often does not induce a groove; small variations in timing qualities, such as syncopation, where accents are shifted in unexpected ways, add complexity to rhythms that help capture embodied reactions to beats.

Rhythmic movement in humans is highly social, and it need not involve musical rhythm at all. We entrain our speech patterns and synchronize our body movements during conversation. Moreover, groups of interacting people can move together over long timescales that can contribute to an overall sense of flowing with a social partner. These kinds of coordinated phenomena seem to be related to nonverbal vocal behaviors. For example, laughing together can predict how coordinated people are in conversation, and the degree of coordination can be related to various measures of feelings of closeness and cooperation. Researchers examining interpersonal coordination in communication use sophisticated techniques incorporating dynamical systems analyses revealing synchrony on multiple timescales, all likely related to an overall subjective sense of being in the groove, or flowing. These perceptions are not linked to our deliberate movements; trying to consciously synch with another in conversation can have negative effects on the actual coordination. People are not typically able to describe verbally what is going on, but they can "feel" it. It is embodied, automatic, and likely an index of how well we might get along outside of the immediate communicative context.

The beat is felt subjectively in the body, and becoming entrained to an isochronous rhythm, especially with other individuals, is a pleasurable goal state that is associated with activity in reward centers of the brain. Moreover, how we encode rhythm is affected by our bodily experience. In one study, researchers bounced babies to an ambiguous auditory rhythm with bouncing accents on either a double or triple beat. They then played the recordings back to the infants days later and found that the babies preferred to listen to auditory analogs of versions that matched what they had been bounced to. The way the babies experienced the beat with their bodies had an impact on how they encoded the sound. Adults even seek out rhythm in noise that is not recognizable as music. In a study of how music preferences shape particular musical features, sound sequences were presented to listeners in pairs, and listeners had to choose which one they preferred. After many repeated exposures across listeners, preferred sounds were replicated with slight modification (emulating mutation), and dis-preferred sounds were removed (i.e., selected against). Over thousands of generations in this extremely simple evolutionary simulation, rhythmic beats emerged spontaneously. We deeply crave rhythm in the sounds we hear.

Research investigating the experience of musicians getting in the groove reveals that these experiences are multimodal and complex (see Levitin et al., 2018, for a review). One of the best signs for musicians that they are in the groove is when the coordinated playing becomes automatic and effortless, and there is a kind of locked performance. Musicians seek out these kinds of experiences, and many report a sustained groove as the height of musical pleasure as a performer. During playing, minor adjustments (i.e., error corrections) are typically needed as the collective performance unfolds in time. The groove emerges dynamically as these errors are resolved, and constant feedback between musicians is often helpful. These adjustments of course often happen mostly unconsciously, but can also involve verbal instruction, nonverbal signals, and musical indicators of success and failure. The direct connection to interpersonal interaction in conversation is fairly straightforward, as conversation is likely the primordial behavior from which culturally evolved musical interaction is derived.

If our ability to entrain is deeply rooted in our sensorimotor experience, and is intricately tied to basic communicative behavior, it is rather easy to understand why cultural processes have been attracted to it. We are highly motivated to engage in musical activity, whether as players, listeners, or dancers. The intense and universal motivation to participate in musical activity suggests social function. Music and other cultural practices that incorporate rhythm are successful because of our embodied predilections. But what social functions could this serve? One possibility is that rhythm provides a means by which groups of people can communicate their social coalitions. Isochronous beat structures allow groups to integrate complex musical and dancing activity in ways that reveal sophisticated and well-rehearsed coordination. The ethnographic record of traditional societies around the world shows clearly that musical performances are very common during initial encounters between distinct groups. These acts, in conjunction with other cultural behaviors, can help groups signal the quality of their relationships, including honest signaling of time spent investing in the performances and the strength of their coalition. Evolution could have favored rhythmic abilities in modern humans beyond those needed for vocal learning, resulting in one of a handful of musical behavioral adaptations that coevolved with cultural traditions.

Ongoing research is looking at many different aspects of this widespread phenomenon, including comparative work attempting to disentangle the evolutionary roots of entrainment and psychological research exploring the complexities of rhythmic coproduction and perception. The topic of rhythm is one that lies at the complex interface of biological and cultural evolution, and much remains to be discovered. We are just now getting in the groove.

For Sources and Further Reading

Levitin, D. J., Grahn, J. A., & London, J. (2018). The psychology of music: Rhythm and movement. *Annual Review of Psychology, 69*, 51–75.

Phillips-Silver, J., Aktipis, C. A., & Bryant, G. A. (2010). The ecology of entrainment: Foundations of coordinated rhythmic movement. *Music Perception: An Interdisciplinary Journal, 28*(1), 3–14.

Ravignani, A., Bowling, D. L., & Fitch, W. (2014). Chorusing, synchrony, and the evolutionary functions of rhythm. *Frontiers in Psychology, 5*, 1118.

Project website: where rhythm emerges in an evolutionary simulation: http://darwintunes.org/

11 The Embodiment of Emotion

Giovanna Colombetti

Emotions are cognitive in that they involve some level of understanding of what is going on in the world or in one's own body. The cognitive nature of the emotions, however, does not imply that they are merely "brainy." Brain and body are deeply interrelated, and emotions should therefore be regarded as thoroughly embodied.

We live in the age of the brain. As Fernando Vidal and Francisco Ortega argue in their 2017 book *Being Brains: Making the Cerebral Subject*, we identify our subjectivity with brain processes. We think that we are fundamentally our brains. A related aspect of this ideology is that we think that the brain is the powerhouse of the mind. Before you read any further, you may try this: enter "mind" or "cognition" into Google Images. Done? What did you find? Most probably pictures of heads and brains – some even projecting light around them, as if the mind were an emanation of energy from the brain. The idea that the mind is in the head, or is caused by the brain, or literally *is* the brain is deeply entrenched in our culture. It is apparent also in the conversational gesture of pointing to one's forehead to refer to the activity of thinking. And as a lecturer, I have noted that my students often (and increasingly) use "brain-talk" to describe how they feel or think, often saying things like: "my brain is not very quick today," or "I don't understand, my brain is hurting!"

At the same time, we are also intimately familiar with mental states that clearly appear to involve the *body* (for expository purposes, "body" here refers specifically to organs and processes located in the biological organism outside the brain). These mental states are our *emotions*: fear, anger, joy, sadness, jealousy, disgust, embarrassment, and so on. When we are in an emotional state, we often display characteristic facial expressions and other behaviors (we cry when sad, blush when embarrassed, tense up when angry, etc.). We also *feel* our body changing. For instance, we experience our heart beating fast when we are agitated or angry, for example, before speaking in public or if someone aggressively accuses us. It is difficult to imagine having an emotion without the body undergoing any change or without feeling any bodily sensation. Famously, the philosopher William James thought this was actually *impossible*. In a much-debated article published in 1884, he claimed that a purely disembodied emotion is a nonentity – it cannot exist. If you take the body away from an emotion, all you are left with is a feelingless state of "cold cognition."

Contemporary philosophers and psychologists recognize that the body is often involved in emotion. However, they emphasize that emotions are primarily *cognitive* mental states: Emotions include cognition – that is, knowledge or understanding (from the Latin *cognoscere*: to know, to come to know, to judge). In particular, contemporary theorists emphasize that emotions involve cognitive judgments and evaluations (also called "appraisals"). Being scared or agitated before speaking in public, for example, is said to involve the appraisal that one might say silly things, or be ill-judged by others; being sad and worried when not finding one's cat involves the judgment that the cat is valuable to one, that she might be hurt, and so on.

It is certainly important to stress that emotions are cognitive. In the history of emotion theory, however, this claim has often led to dismissing and side-lining the body. Psychological and philosophical accounts popular in the 60s and 70s illustrate this phenomenon well. In those years the body was often regarded as neither sufficient nor necessary for emotion. In other words, emotions were conceived of as *entirely* cognitive or "brainy" (as cognition was, and still is, generally regarded as taking place entirely in the brain). The fact that one's heart accelerates before speaking in public was seen as a mere contingent concomitant of fear; that is, such reactions are something that happens, sometimes or even often, but that does not *have* to happen for fear to occur – one would still be scared as long as one judged that speaking in public is scary.

The situation is different today, as most emotion theorists and affective scientists conceive of emotions as *both* cognitive and bodily. They regard cognitive appraisals *as well as* various bodily changes (in facial and vocal expression, posture, behavior, autonomic nervous system activity) as central aspects, or "components," of emotion. This view does not imply that every emotional episode must come with changes in *all* of these components. The claim is, rather, that changes in these components are typical of the clearest cases of emotion.

Is it accurate to say, then, that affective scientists today regard emotions as embodied mental states rather than as merely brainy ones? Well, yes and no. Yes, because, as just noted, they often regard bodily changes as typical components of emotions, next to cognitive/brain components. No, however, because the role they assign to the body in emotion is still secondary and ancillary to the one of cognition and the brain. In a nutshell: The body has been reinstated in emotion theory, but it still does not have the same status of the brain.

This situation can be seen as yet another manifestation of the "ideology of the cerebral subject" denounced by Ortega and Vidal and mentioned at the start. Emotions, many affective scientists insist, are cognitive and therefore intelligent. And where does the intelligence of the emotions reside? In the brain, of course – for where else could it reside, if the brain is considered the seat of cognition? In other words, contemporary affective science recognizes that the body plays an important role in emotion, yet characterizes this role not as one of understanding or making sense of the world, but as a practical one of reacting to stimuli in order to mobilize action. The intelligent work of evaluating the environment remains a prerogative of brain-located cognition.

There are reasons to question this view. A main reason has to do with physiology. The more we know about the workings of the organism, the less the brain appears to be an organ of control, with the body serving merely to keep it alive. What physiology tells us, instead, is that the brain and the body are interrelated in complex ways, at multiple levels and timescales. Given such a deep integration, it is not clear that we can attribute "pure" cognitive functions to the brain only, and noncognitive, simply reactive functions to the body. Relatedly, it is not clear that we can neatly separate the cognitive/brainy components of emotion from the bodily ones.

Take, for example, the case of stress. Many affective scientists regard the brain as the physical basis of emotions. They claim that the brain (or rather specific parts of it) evaluates stimuli in the environment, and subsequently generates or produces corresponding emotions – such as fear in response to (brain-detected) danger, sadness in response to (brain-detected) loss, and so on. Relatedly, they regard stress as a response to brain-detected threat. They also claim that the brain drives and controls the bodily changes that occur as a consequence of the brain evaluating the environment. Both claims are manifestations of a *brainocentric* perspective that privileges the brain over other parts of the organism when explaining how emotions come about and unfold.

When one looks at *physiological* accounts of stress, however, one notes that they have long claimed that various endocrine bodily organs and processes influence how the organism responds to challenging (i.e., stressful) situations. Physiological accounts of stress do not focus on the brain only, but describe how certain parts of the brain (the hypothalamus) interact with endocrine glands located in the body (the pituitary and the adrenal glands) and with the hormones released by these glands (e.g., corticotropic releasing hormone, adrenocorticotropic hormone, glucocorticoids). The standard physiological story is that the brain responds to stressors by releasing hormones that influence endocrine glands in the body, which *in turn* release further hormones that have various effects on *both* body and brain. In humans, the adrenal glands release cortisol – a glucocorticoid that can rapidly reach various bodily organs as well as the brain. Once in the brain, cortisol can influence its own synthesis by inhibiting the secretory activity of the hypothalamus. This negative feedback loop illustrates nicely that it is not just the brain that regulates the body, but also the other way around. This fact alone puts pressure on brainocentrism, because it shows that an emotion such as stress is not adequately characterized solely as a brain process, nor as a brain-body process that is entirely generated and controlled by the brain.

And this is not the end of the story. Further fascinating recent evidence shows that plasma concentration of glucocorticoids oscillates hourly and, moreover, independently of the brain (for details and references, see Colombetti & Zavala, 2019). Importantly for the notion of embodiment, this oscillation dynamically influences how the organism responds to the environment. For example, rats react more aggressively toward a social intruder when their glucocorticoid levels are rising, compared to when they are falling. This evidence challenges brainocentrism further, because it illustrates that stress is not entirely determined and controlled by the brain but depends on bodily processes as well, some of which are even independent from the brain.

Still, this is not *yet* the end of the story – because, in addition, the stress system described so far influences, and is in turn influenced by, various other physiological processes occurring at the level of the immune and the gastrointestinal system, including the gut microbiota (the many different bacteria and other microorganisms that live in the gut). Given this complexity, to say that stress is an emotion generated and controlled by the brain appears decidedly misleading.

What about other emotional states, though? One might think that stress is an exception in its involvement of so many physiological processes. Not so. Evidence is mounting that depression and anxiety, too, recruit specific changes not just in brain neurochemistry but also in endocrine and immune processes, including gut microbiota (see Colombetti & Zavala, 2019, for details). And stress, depression, and anxiety often come together and feed one another, and importantly also influence a range of other emotional states, including short-lived ones. More precisely, stress, anxiety, and depression can be seen as overarching affective conditions that determine the range of emotional responses one is likely to exhibit at any given time – very much like climate zones (e.g., temperate or arid) determine the likelihood of specific local weather patterns (rain, drought, etc.). We also know from experience that being depressed makes one more prone to feeling dejected, hopeless, or guilty; the same stimulus, such as a mild critical remark, will affect a depressed and a nondepressed person differently. Similarly for stress and anxiety.

The upshot is that it seems neither possible nor advisable to regard stress and other emotional states as based entirely or primarily in the brain. Many short-lived emotional responses to stimuli arguably depend on more global, longer-lasting emotional conditions (sometimes also called "moods" and "mood disorders") whose physiological bases straddle mutually influencing brain and bodily processes. And more generally, the brain and body are *always* interacting and influencing one another – not just during stress, anxiety, or depression. Given this integration, it does not seem possible to divide the realm of emotional states into the embodied ones, and the merely brainy ones.

In sum, to regard emotion as properly embodied entails going beyond acknowledging that it involves bodily changes. Embodiment as an alternative to brainocentrism should also challenge the popular assumption that the cognitive or intelligent dimension of emotion depends entirely on the brain. As physiology tells us that the body is so intimately coupled or integrated with the brain, the body then ought not to be seen as a mere reactant. Rather, the body ought to be seen as an active participant in the process of making sense of stimuli and situations beyond its borders.

For Sources and Further Reading

Colombetti, G. (2014). *The feeling body: Affective science meets the enactive mind.* Cambridge: MIT Press.

Colombetti, G., & Zavala, E. (2019). Are emotions based in the brain? A critique of affective brainocentrism from a physiological perspective. *Biology and Philosophy, 34*, 45.

Vidal, F., & Ortega, F. (2017). *Being brains: Making the cerebral subject.* New York: Fordham University Press.

12 Body Focus in Expert Action

Barbara Gail Montero, John Toner and Aidan Moran

Although adopting an explicit, conscious "body focus" may, at times, hinder performance and impede improvement, such a focus may often be advantageous to both practice and performance in highly skilled bodily activities. Empirical studies suggest that certain groups of experts frequently employ bodily foci and that a body focus can help fend off "choking under pressure." Because experts push themselves to achieve their personal best and because bodies and environments are labile, a body focus may be needed to control action.

Achieving a desired goal that is just out of reach may sometimes require focusing on the *means* rather than the end. For example, if an aspiring thief wants to steal Vincent van Gogh's "The Starry Night," from the Museum of Modern Art, the thief needs to find a disguise, gather tools, arrange for a getaway car, and so forth. But stealing second base in a baseball game, some claim, is not like this: A runner on first base who is focusing on the means of stealing second – specifically, the *bodily* means – will soon be out. Indeed, even prior to a nighttime heist, a prospective buyer might caution the thief against concentrating on finger movements while disabling the security system. Although focusing on the means may sometimes be needed to achieve an end, it is thought that focusing on the bodily means is unhelpful.

In sport, many studies suggest that focusing on the body leads to poorer performance relative to focusing on the consequences of bodily actions (see Wulf, 2013, for a review). Indeed, those studies led Wulf (2016) to conclude that "if movements are not planned in terms of the intended movement effect, but in terms of specific body movements, the outcome will always be less-than-optimal" (p. 338, cited in Montero et al., 2018). We do not doubt that there are times in an athlete's, dancer's, or other professional mover's career when adopting an explicit, conscious "body focus" may hinder performance and impede improvement. And whether athletes are always marginally aware of their bodies (a topic beyond the scope of this essay) deserves attention. However, we shall present some reasons to think that in highly skilled bodily activities, it is often advantageous – both to practice and performance – to adopt an explicit bodily focus.

Let's begin with an obvious example of where a bodily focus is necessary for achieving one's goals: The small subset of skills whose success conditions are, at least in part, defined in terms of attaining a bodily-centered focus. The dance practice Gaga is illustrative (see Katan-Schmid, 2016, cited in Montero et al., 2018). As Gaga is concerned not with how you look but with how you *feel*, you are sometimes asked to focus on very specific parts of the body, such as the webbing between your fingers. Other activities that explicitly require a body focus are certain types of yoga and meditation where the point is to focus on one's breathing. Because an explicit aim of these activities is to focus on the body, failing to do so, in these activities, means failing to perform optimally.

That such skills are aided by a bodily focus is uncontroversial. However, we argue that even beyond this small subset of skills, athletes and others whose skills are body based can sometimes benefit from focusing on the movements of their bodies.

One important reason why adopting a body focus can, at times, be beneficial to a wide range of skills is that focusing on one's body can promote conscious control. The relevance of conscious control to improved skill might seem straightforward: Put simply, to fine tune your actions, you need to control them consciously. However, the empirical evidence does not invariably support this position. Wulf and Lewthwaite (2010, cited in Montero et al., 2018), for example, argue that in expert skill, a conscious mode of control may trigger self-evaluative and self-regulatory processing which may result in "choking" episodes (a sudden deterioration in skilled performance due to anxiety). Although we think that conscious control may sometimes impede certain skills, we are not convinced that it is *always* harmful. In fact, we believe that a body focus can sometimes be used to prevent choking. We believe that body focus may be helpful, in part, because even highly practiced skills might not be fully automated (Carr, 2015). Experts frequently try to push themselves to achieve their "personal best," to shave off a couple seconds in a cross-country race or make the ending of a pirouette more seamless. And, as noted by Ericsson and colleagues (1993, cited in Montero, 2018), going beyond what you have done involves leaving the comfort zone of automaticity.

Furthermore, environments are often labile and every day the body is slightly different, and slight differences may matter for the exacting and extremely important skills that an athlete or dancer may enact. As the tennis player Rafael Nadal put it in his 2011 book (with Carlin), *Rafa*, "every day you wake up feeling differently . . . [and] every shot is different"; thus, even after hitting millions of balls, "hitting a true, smooth clean shot every time . . . [is not] a piece of cake" (p. 132). And if a challenge is present, we suggest, you need conscious attention. You might not need conscious attention to your bodily movements; however, as we shall go on to argue, in at least some cases of expert action, a body focus is beneficial.

There is evidence from empirical studies that certain groups of experts frequently employ bodily foci. When Guss-West and Wulf (2016) surveyed 53 international professional ballet dancers to identify what these performers focused on or imagined when preparing and executing a variety of actions, they found that 72% of responses related to body movements, and sometimes even quite specific, low-level bodily movements. For example, when describing the type of focus they adopted during a *grand jete* (a large leap), the dancers reported, among other things, focusing on the "gluteal engagement of the push off leg for thrust" and "releasing the air from my lungs to prevent the shoulders from going up; turning the head to the public," while balancing in arabesque, where a dancer stands on pointe on one leg and extends the other leg high into the air behind her, the dancers' reports included "feeling my center controlled over my supporting leg" and "the big toe of my arabesque floating away and up." Conceivably, such a focus may have no effect on their movements. The widespread use of body focus among professional dancers, however, indicates that it may be beneficial. Using a similar approach, Stoate and Wulf (2011, cited in Montero et al., 2018) found that a number of expert swimmers reported focusing on their bodies – focusing, for example, on "high elbow," "pull hands back," "hip rotation" – when asked to adopt their "normal" focus of attention. Yet they also found that this body focus proved optimal for some swimmers but less than optimal for others.

By focusing on their bodies, athletes and others might focus directly, via proprioception, on a muscle or joint to fine-tune control or to monitor an injury (Montero, 2018). But, arguably, experts may also find it useful to focus on the body indirectly via imagery. Bernier et al. (2016, cited in Toner et al., forthcoming) found that skaters used visual and kinaesthetic images before, and indeed during, some of their jumps. One skater reported, "During the approach to the jump, actually, I'm doing the jump in my head: I have the same sensations in my body, and I feel like I'm doing it in my upper body and hips;" another revealed that: "Here, when I place my foot to take off, I have an image in my head that my neck is really straight... My coach, when I was young, he told me to picture a hair standing straight up, perpendicular to the top of my head. So here, I'm visualizing this image" (p. 261). In these examples, it seems that bodily foci, mediated through mental imagery, assist performance perhaps by focusing the mind and heightening control.

Apart from the ability to facilitate conscious control over one's movements, adopting a body focus has been seen as beneficial in alleviating anxiety, which is a crucial trigger of choking episodes (Hill & Hemmings, 2015). One way that anxiety distracts one from one's optimal focus is by turning one's mind to disturbing thoughts about such things as what others will think, or the possibility of failure or, indeed, how much the mind is racing and not focusing on what is important (Wine, 1971, cited in Montero et al., 2018). And although the best way to cope with anxiety is very much an open question, some athletes manage it by focusing on the details of their bodily movements. For example, in Hill et al.'s (2010, cited in Hill & Hemmings, 2015) study on choking under pressure, some golfers claimed that focusing more on their skills helped *prevent* a more severe performance breakdown.

Although some of the warnings against body focus apply not just to performance but to practice as well (Wulf, 2016), there seem to be strong reasons to think that both body focus and a disruption of automaticity can be useful in practice. According to Anders Ericsson's theory of deliberate practice (Ericsson et al., 1993), automaticity leads to stagnation: Performing automatically may help maintain a level of performance but will not allow improvement. Thus, if adopting a body focus can lead to consciously controlling a movement, such foci in practice can leave to door open to continued improvement. And when an athlete or dancer has been applying a body focus during practice, a bodily focus would be natural and thus one would not expect it to hinder performance. As Maurer and Munzert (2013) found in their study of skilled basketball players' focus during free throw performance, irrespective of focus direction (internal or external), "frequently used familiar focus strategies become integrated into the proceduralized skill components and are no longer disruptive to skill execution" (p. 737, cited in Montero et al., 2018). Furthermore, a body focus can also be pleasurable, and thus would encourage prolonged practice.

Finally, although numerous studies appear to support the view that focusing on the body leads to suboptimal results, the long-term effect of focusing on one's body is untested empirically. And this is significant because, as Peh et al. (2011, cited in Montero et al., 2018) suggest, it could be that the most effective training schedule can disrupt performance in the short-run while it improves it over a longer period of time. It is also quite difficult to design experiments that adequately investigate how adopting a body focus affects skill even in the short run. This is so because it is challenging to design experiments to test body and external foci that are balanced both in terms of how natural or familiar an expert finds them and in terms of their relevancy to the task. We hope that future research into body focus will be able to address these shortcomings.

In Memoriam

We (B. G. M. and J. T.) note with sorrow the passing of our colleague, Aidan Moran, who died shortly after this essay was completed. We are richer for having known and worked with him, and the scholarly community is richer for his contributions.

For Sources and Further Reading

Carr, T. H. (2015). Strengths and weaknesses of reflection as a guide to action: Pressure assails performance in multiple ways. *Phenomenology and the Cognitive Sciences, 14*, 227–252.

Guss-West, C., & Wulf, G. (2016). Attentional focus in classical ballet: A survey of professional dancers. *Journal of Dance Medicine & Science, 20*(1), 23–29.

Hill, D. M., & Hemmings, B. (2015). A phenomenological exploration of coping responses associated with choking in sport. *Qualitative Research in Sport, Exercise and Health, 7*(4), 521–538.

Montero, B. G. (2018). *Thought in action: Expertise and the conscious mind.* Oxford: Oxford University Press.

Montero, B. G., Toner, J., & Moran, A. (2018). Questioning the breadth of the external focus effect. In M. L. Cappuccio (Ed.), *Handbook of embodied cognition and sport psychology* (pp. 199–221). Cambridge: MIT Press.

Toner, J., Montero, B. G., & Moran, A. (forthcoming). *Continuous improvement in elite performance.* Oxford, UK: Oxford University Press.

Wulf, G. (2013). Attentional focus and motor learning: A review of 15 years. *International Review of Sport and Exercise Psychology, 6*(1), 77–104.

Part IV
(Re)Locating

In what way do eddies, ebbs, and flows of varied, sensuous bodies collectively comprise human sociopolitical organization and spatial distribution? How does the cultural and geographical positioning of bodies stunt or nurture, constrain or liberate, upset or settle them? The essays in this section take up these questions, making the case for incorporation of other-than-discursive processes of human life into multiplex understandings of subordination and dislocation and fresh imaginings of just societies.

13 How Bodies Become Viscous

Arun Saldanha

The embodied perspective departs from an individualist and mentalist way of understanding the social. The basic argument is that
the "body politic" (governments, social movements, corporations)
consists of the largely unconscious sticking together of bodies according to their differences.

While sensory perception and bodily location have been extensively
conceptualized, what happens when many bodies come together *as
bodies* has mostly escaped attention in social theorizing. This essay
discusses four dimensions of human bodies: sensuousness, variation, locatedness, and viscosity. The embodied perspective departs
from an individualist and mentalist way of understanding the social. The basic argument is that the "body politic" (governments,
social movements, corporations) consists of the largely unconscious
sticking together of bodies *according to* their differences. Viscosity
refers to this dynamic emergence, at scales from the street to the
planet, of collectivities of people based on corporeal attributes.

Sensuous Bodies

Embodiment has until recently been neglected by social theorists
more or less in line with the foundational Western philosophical
expunging of emotions and the flesh. Descartes and Newton epito-
mized scientific positivism, striving for ostensibly objective and dis-
interested knowledge at the expense of the immediate relationships
the senses develop with their surroundings. What difference does
it make to call social phenomena embodied? Firstly, an insistence
on sensory perception highlights certain crucial components that
are more often than not obliterated from purview for ideological
reasons. For example, the nation-state is often embodied through

physical violence and pain (and their painful recollections). The importance of rape for ethnic cleansing and warfare has until recently escaped attention. Secondly, the cultural reproduction of geopolitical relations and entities (through parades or border patrol) can be more concretely studied if what bodies do and feel enters the discussion. Thirdly, the affective qualities of leaders and rhetoric, circulating within constituencies, can be meticulously analyzed as legible corporeal signs (think of Hitler's body language). Fourthly, more and more geopolitics itself depends on the biometrical management of bodies through what Michel Foucault called *biopolitics*. What many are arguing in the wake of Foucault is that the intrusion of the state into the biological being of people (refugees, convicts, citizens) is accompanied by a whole new range of emotions and embodied skills. If it seeks to understand the concrete nature of these political changes, social theory has to take into account their targets and vehicles: bodies of flesh, blood, senses, genes, and memories.

Different Bodies

Embodiment is fundamentally about difference. Feminist politics therefore starts with the difference between women and men. All of Western thought has not only overwhelmingly been conjured by men, among men, and for men, but these men have also always talked on behalf of everyone else: women, children, slaves, foreigners, the Indigenous, the old, and the sick. The philosophy of Luce Irigaray exposes the implicit privileging in European philosophy of the average male body and its particular morphology. The specific characteristics of femininity and masculinity have been consistently ignored in the centuries-old conceptualization of "man." Irigaray's ethics and politics follow from what she sees as the irreducibility of sexual difference. Biology is then not destiny, but the playground for ethical and political experimentation.

The sensual and differential nature of bodies needs to be seen as *a question of many bodies.* How to conceive of collective embodiment from the street to the continental has not been satisfactorily explored. We hear of "the body" but seldom about bodies. This *de facto* methodological individualism is foreign to the life sciences. In population biology and biogeography species and subspecies groups do not have essences but are dynamic outcomes of many interacting organisms. Evolution itself is understood as the net effects of many organisms adapting to their changing environments.

So both biologically and culturally, embodiment is *already* differentiated. Every human accumulates tastes, attitudes, habits, and gestures. A human body develops as it goes to certain places and engages with things and other bodies. How does voting behavior differentiate populations through collective fear? How many protesters can move through a street without getting clogged up? Whose senses will likely to be stirred by populist propaganda? The challenge is to think of those populations not as mere "minds," decisions, or sets of data, but as thinking and feeling organisms continually on the move, mixing with each other in certain physical settings.

Located Bodies

Bodies differ not just anatomically, neurologically, and medically. Bodies always exist *somewhere*. What bodies can do depends on their location in uneven distributions of resources and media imageries, and deeper, as the Indian Ocean tsunami and New Orleans flood showed, in seismic and climate processes. What matters is one's position in all the constellations that human and physical geographers map. Feminists have taken up location to describe how uneven development and socio-spatial boundaries delimit choices, and more so for women than men, more so for the poor and the black than for the white and wealthy. Black, immigrant, diasporic, and third world feminists have emphasized the tremendous importance of bodily specificity to the politics of location so that the exploration of location multiplied feminism itself. Doreen Massey argued for decades that space itself is constructed differentially. Globalization affects and is affected by different groups in glaringly different ways, according to what Massey called *power-geometries.*

It is *because* bodies vary sexually, racially, and economically that they get differently located in geographies of power and possibility. The sensuous, voluminous materiality of phenotypes should be explored as expressions of global capitalism and colonialism. It is not simply a question of bodies being "inscribed" by geography, but geography materially constituting bodies and their capacities. This is evident in the geographies of food. Anyone's diet reproduces class- and race-based tastes and health disparities, and there is a growing awareness of the effects of consumption on ecosystems and vulnerable populations both human and nonhuman, especially of meat. But how bodies relate to social space can also be imagined in the geographies of education or religion. When trained as an electrician, one literally incorporates and transports certain skills; when facing Mecca one literally aligns one's body with millions of others.

It is equally crucial to understand, conversely, that location does not follow deterministically from phenotypic particularity. How a body is intercepted by global flows depends on what bodily features matter in everyday interaction and in the reproduction of social relations and institutions. Sexual and racial segregation shows that it is the materiality of bodies itself that makes particular spatialities endure, though the segregation follows contingently from the interplay of urban planning, architecture, surveillance cameras, urinals, and so on. Bodies are not blank surfaces. Their genitals, hair, and health need to be molded and charged by power-geometries; they need to be pushed and pulled to certain places. There is no social inequality without the affective and monetary investment in the shifting particularities of bodies.

Viscous Bodies

Whether human or not, many bodies together are very rarely chaotic. They are capable of "communicating" movement to each other, becoming sticky relative to one another, even if they keep moving and remain a plurality. This process of becoming-sticky is what I have called *viscosity*. The concept has an affinity with the better-known term in science of *emergence*, the spontaneous appearance of coherent group motion irreducible to what the many particles do individually. Viscosity is inevitably about a multiplicity of elements, and one can appreciate the many-ness of viscosity only in physical terms. A classic example is the relative unison of flying birds. The bird bodies stick together as a temporary system, yet remain many, flying in order to avoid their neighbors. Viscosity wants to emphasize this mobile spatiality of togetherness, of coordinated flowing and relative stability. Unlike gases, viscous liquids do not move randomly; unlike solids, they are not static.

Viscosity is more than a metaphor. It does not only apply to fluids or birds. Human flows become viscous in crowds, in large airports, and in traffic jams. Crowds are easily appreciated as being sticky because they are about concentration in one place. But human bodies stick together in more durable ways: packs, crowds, cities, nation-states, social classes, Facebook groups, and racial formations. If thinking the viscosity of bodies on scales larger than the city is difficult, this only proves how unaccustomed we are to thinking bodies *as bodies,* as shifting and linked masses subject to gravity and expulsion. Viscosity is a quintessentially spatial process, but it need not depend on either geographical proximity or actual deceleration. It is about flows and networks, and how they intersect, before it is about places. Remember that the flock of birds can be both moving erratically in real space and remaining viscous in topological terms.

Philip Ball usefully summarizes recent advances in what he hopes will be a "physics of society." Strange as it may seem, Ball's book is in effect a physicist's answer to Hobbesian political philosophy. While rejecting Hobbes' bleak assumption of human selfishness, Ball revives the early-modern enthusiasm of approaching human aggregation physically, like grains of sand or droplets of water. Of course, it is today's powerful computation technology that enables the probing into the mathematical depths of collective behavior. It is far from certain to what extent computer modeling of complex behavior hints at physical *laws* shared by humans and everything else. What is more certain is that much of contemporary physics, like biology, is less mechanistic and positivist than social theory makes of it. On a par with Irigaray, science after complexity theory can grapple with the *creativity* of bodies.

If the sticking-together of crowds in public space is relatively easy to appreciate, a brief elaboration on the viscosity of racial formations will allow for imagining what the concept can do for theorizing society. Population geography demonstrates that migration (e.g., during the European colonial era) follows spatial *patterns.* Indigenous populations remain in a certain region for many centuries, though more often than not were displaced by colonialism. Other populations emigrate in large numbers, go on holiday, or maintain networks of diasporic kinship. Within countries, within cities, these populations furthermore coalesce in certain landscapes, neighborhoods, churches, or camps. This whole host of degrees of movement and stasis is what the concept of viscosity tries to designate. However, the concept demands in addition that we imagine the phenotypic, sensory, and cultural specificity of these masses of bodies: their skin color, diet, health, reproduction rate, religious affects. And there are bodies even more difficult to map: business travelers, for example, who are usually white, male, heterosexual, and able-bodied. Through their high mobility, businessmen keep corporate capitalism and patriarchal power-geometries in place. In the framework of viscosity, the *formation* of racial difference becomes a literal term, an extremely complex configuration of bodies moving on a range of scales with a range of speeds, with shapes that can only be approximated in maps.

The political upshot of thinking social collectivities and the body politic as sensuous, differential, located, and viscous is that exchanges are possible between the so-called "social" and the "natural" sciences with an eye on bringing clarification to how inequalities come about and sustain themselves. The intellectual resources for such a project are, as this essay shows, multiple and sometimes at odds with one another. The theme of embodiment cannot but raise scholars from their disciplinary slumber.

For Sources and Further Reading

Ball, P. (2004). *Critical mass: How one thing leads to another.* London: Arrow Books.

Massey, D. (1994). *Space, place, and gender.* Minneapolis: University of Minnesota Press.

Saldanha, A. (2007). *Psychedelic white: Goa trance and the viscosity of race.* Minneapolis: University of Minnesota Press.

Saldanha, A. (2008). The political geography of many bodies. In K. R. Cox, M. Low, & J. Robinson (Eds.), *The Sage handbook of political geography* (pp. 323–334). London: Sage. Note: The current essay is a strongly abridged and modified version of this chapter.

Slocum, R. & Saldanha, A. (Eds.). (2013). *Geographies of race and food: Fields, bodies, markets.* Farnham, UK: Ashgate.

Young, I. M. (1990). *Throwing like a girl and other essays in feminist philosophy and social theory.* Bloomington: Indiana University Press.

14 Embodiment, Plasticity, Biosociality, and Epigenetics

The Politics of a Vulnerable Body for Toxic Times

Maurizio Meloni

The complex links between social structures and biological bodies are increasingly recognized. The field of epigenetics offers scientific evidence about the "biological embedding" of social experience – how environmental factors can be inscribed on the biological body. However, the social implications of epigenetics for race, class, and gender inequalities have to be addressed carefully.

While ideas of embodiment are far from new and go back in the West to the Hippocratic treatise on Airs, Waters, and Places in the 5th/4th century BCE, modern biomedical views, and genetics in particular, have traditionally sidelined this ecological line of thought. Biomedical thought in the 20th century has mostly foregrounded internal factors, such as genes, as the root of health trajectories. Significantly, this line of thought has tended to clearly separate biological from social factors, postulating the latter intervene at some secondary time to alter or interact with the capacity of the first. The last three decades have witnessed a significant questioning of this approach. As reviewed in *Impressionable Biologies* (Meloni, 2019), a wealth of evidence has emerged on the complex pathways that link social experience to biology, health and disease risk, opening up questions on the separation of biological and social factors.

At the level of the individual body, data from neuroimmunological research and neuroscience have highlighted the dependence of neuroendocrine and immune functions on social and psychological processes. The emphasis has been on how socio-economic status and social structures – such as the qualities of neighborhoods and communities, or social isolation – may have a profound impact on brain development and functioning and patterns of morbidity and mortality (Cacioppo & Patrick, 2008). Moving from the individual body to what Stuckler and Basu (2013) call the "body economic," an increasing number of studies now focus on the way in which austerity policies and inequalities are literally *killing factors*. As Krieger argued in *Epidemiology and People's Health* (2011), these recent works can be better appreciated within the context of a longer tradition of social epidemiology research on how inequality, discrimination, and racism literally harm health, producing different population patterns of disease distribution.

Epigenetics and Embodiment: Deepening the Agenda

A framework rooted in *biological embedding* – to use Clyde Hertzman's term – posits that the biological body bears the inscriptions of its lived experience and its social and material contexts, and these contexts are constituted by the socially modulated biographies of the body, past and present (toxic exposures, dietary factors, financial and educational capital, social networks). *Epigenetics* has raised hope and expectations that it could provide this debate on how environmental factors get under the skin and are inscribed on the biological body with crucial, and so far missing, molecular evidence. Epigenetics describes changes to the chemical structure of DNA triggered by environmental cues. These changes alter gene and phenotypic expression of an organism without change to DNA base-pair sequences.

Coined by British embryologist and polymath C. H. Waddington (1905–1975) in the 1940s, epigenetics was originally meant as a neologism from *epigenesis* (not "on the top of" or "above genes" as in today's folk etymology) to define in a broader nonmolecular sense an interdisciplinary study of all the "causal interactions between genes and their products which bring the phenotype into being" (Waddington, 1942, cited in Meloni, 2019). Since the early 2000s, epigenetics has turned into a burgeoning subbranch of molecular biology where the developmental complexity that links genes and environments to phenotypes is investigated at the molecular level. *DNA methylation* is the most recognized and studied of these molecular mechanisms of epigenetic mutation. The term refers to the addition of a methyl group to a DNA base, resulting in inhibition of gene transcription. It is often dependent on nutritional or wider extra-cellular factors, giving a wider dynamism to genetic functioning.

Michael Meaney's experiments on the transmission of poor maternal care in rats well illustrate this dynamism of the genome via methylation changes, where wider social signals regulate the organism physiology. Certain behavioral exposures (low licking/

grooming by the mother rat, or *dam*) shape changes in methyla-tion patterns in offspring that alter genetic expression and hence long-term neurochemical responses in the brain. This modifies the physiology of the pups, who, as adults, will reproduce the inducing behavior and consequently modify their environmental niche, thus shaping the biological life also of a next generation. Importantly, cross-fostering pups to high licking/grooming dams reversed the methylation pattern (Weaver et al., 2004, cited in Meloni, 2016).

Although epigenetics is often described as the fifth letter of the linear genetic code, it is better understood as an environmentally driven change to chromatin, the macromolecule into which DNA fibers are folded, comprising chromosomes (see Meloni, 2019, for more detail). In a nutshell and at the cost of simplification, DNA is structurally constrained by chromatin architecture and this ar-chitecture can be remodeled partly in response to environmental inputs. Chromatin strands can be transcriptionally "open," and thus potentially expressed, or "closed," and thus silenced by wider cellular and extra-cellular signals. The flexible rearrangement of chromatin structure enables the dynamic interplay between gene functions and the environment, and more broadly organism and milieu over the lifespan. As a regulator of the chromatin system, epigenetics constitutes a significant opportunity to reconceptualize embodiment in a way that includes genetics factors. However, the so-called *post-genomic genome* is no longer seen in the driving seat of biological processes. Rather, it has to be understood as embed-ded into a context-dependent regulative framework, described as highly sensitive and responsive to environmental influences, plastic to social effects and cues. It has become a *biosocial genome*, to use Müller and colleagues' (2017) term. This line of investigation highly complicates the neat distinction between biological and social fac-tors, calling increasingly for a "biology of social causes" and a "so-ciology of biological effects." It is at this level that the debates on biosocial models of health and disease or biological plasticity have attracted increasing interest and may become an important plat-form for cross-disciplinary collaborations across the social/natural science divide.

Epigenetics in Toxic Times: A Politics of Vulnerable Bodies

The reassuring fiction of a DNA segregated from experiential factors, which translates into reassuring disciplinary boundaries between nature-oriented and culture-oriented disciplines, may be a luxury we cannot afford anymore given the ubiquitous toxicity of life in the Anthropocene. Epigenetic changes are likely to be studied as an archive or a biomarker of toxic exposures that, especially in crucial key windows of development (in utero, early life, adolescence, pregnancy), may materialize as a morbid alteration to present and future health trajectories. A small but growing body of literature has also highlighted the potential multigenerational effects of poisoned exposures, either to stress, famine, or social exploitation and violence.

The policy implications of these emerging findings, however, present a number of ethical and social dilemmas that need to be addressed carefully. Care is particularly important because there is a long (albeit often forgotten) history of eugenic and racist policies based on the belief that heredity is not fixed at birth but influenced by the environment and hence bad environments result in damaged people (Meloni, 2016). For instance, if the effects of a future parent's diet on offspring's wellbeing are validated by epigenetic findings, how does this change notions of responsibility and risk, normality and pathology? If the genome can be damaged by smoking or optimized through exercise, will we not – as White and Wastell (2016) suggest – monitor individual lifestyles more carefully than ever? In this way, aren't lifestyle and behavioral structures increasingly burdened with biomedical implications and hence normative demands? What about recent popular and scientific claims that people are "poisoned" or "marked for life" by bad environments? Will this lead to claims about social justice and reparation or an identification of vulnerable groups as "at greater risk" and hence open to new types of regulation, policy and medical surveillance?

The recent epigenetic and developmentalist argument that racial differences in health are not the product of a set of inherited genes but the biological embedding of common exposures to racialized structures and social gradients of stress (Kuzawa & Sweet, 2009, cited in Meloni, 2016) may legitimize the notion that there is, after all, a biological meaning to race. Moreover, if people embody their toxic environments in this linear way, and if some of these effects may travel across a certain number of generations, what are policymakers supposed to do with this notion? Offer compensation or reparation for what has occurred in the past and still haunt the biology of contemporary generations? Or instead, as it occurred in past eugenics arguments, use this notion to claim that certain groups are too damaged (not by faulty genes but by toxic histories) to deserve a substantial financial or educational investment for their future? And what about the gender inequality of epigenetic effects, given that women embody their surrounding environments in a more direct way, especially during pregnancy? Might they not be increasingly encouraged by developmental models to plan the health of their offspring well before conception – and to be expected to do so by others – which is a burden not equally borne by men? Finally, what sort of embodiment is epigenetics promoting? One where people are just seen as the passive receivers, not this time of DNA signals but of environmental exposures? How can ideas of agency and vitality be rescued in this model?

These dilemmas do not mean that research in epigenetics will necessarily be hijacked into racialist or sexist political agendas. However, they should sound a warning that views of embodiment and ecologies of the body are not necessarily simplistically aligned with politically progressive views.

For Sources and Further Reading

Cacioppo, J., & Patrick, B. (2008). *Loneliness: Human nature and the need for social connection*. New York: Norton & Company.

Krieger, N. (2011). *Epidemiology and people's health: Theory and context*. New York: Oxford University Press.

Meloni, M. (2016). *Political biology: Science and social values in human heredity from eugenics to epigenetics*. London: Palgrave.

Meloni, M. (2019). *Impressionable biologies: From the archaeology of plasticity to the sociology of epigenetics*. New York: Routledge.

Müller, R., Hanson, C., Hanson, M., Penkler, M., Samaras, G., Chiapperino, L., ... Villa, P. (2017). The biosocial genome? *EMBO Reports, 18*, 1677–1682.

Stuckler, D., & Basu, S. (2013) *The body economic: Why austerity kills*. London: Allen Lane.

White, S. J., & Wastell, D. G. (2016). Epigenetics prematurely born(e): Social work and the malleable gene. *British Journal of Social Work, 47*(8), 2256–2272.

15 Violating the Inviolable

Evolved Reproductive Prerogatives of Individual Women

Patricia Adair Gowaty

Abortion bans defy the inviolability of women's reproductive decision-making, which was ultimately organized by the evolutionary rules of within-sex selection and sexual conflict during the hundreds of millions of years of mammalian evolution.

The current intensification of efforts in the US to curtail women's reproductive rights is not just a horrific political moment, but also a profound evolutionary selection pressure with implications for all of humanity. Here, I describe why the modern efforts to criminalize women who seek medical abortion not only violate the autonomy of individual women but importantly increase the likelihood of deleterious evolutionary results for women, men, and children. In doing so, I connect key concepts of evolution with the insights of ancient and modern feminisms having to do with the political orders of societies, an effort I promoted in the 1990s when writing about the relationships between evolutionary ideas and feminism: I said then and observe now that "Women's oppression is the first, most widespread, and deepest oppression...sexist oppression is fundamental to – is 'the root' of – all other systems of oppression" (1992, p. 219). Today I argue that contemporary efforts criminalizing abortion violate the inviolable and will reduce the lifespan and reproductive success of all – men as well as women. Women's autonomy is an imperative evolved over millions of years of evolutionary sorting. This means that the criminalization of women doing anything to their own bodies is itself a crime against nature. Stopping gestation is a woman's prerogative, not just because gestation is a function of her body including her autonomous decisions about her health, but because of the forces of evolution.

Humans are embodied mammals whose evolutionary divergence from reptiles and birds began hundreds of millions of years ago.

The defining adaptations of modern mammals are that females give birth to live young after a period of internal gestation, which is then followed by provisioning to otherwise helpless offspring of mothers' breast milk from mammary glands that evolved from sweat glands. All mammal mothers including human mothers physiologically control (consciously or unconsciously) the viability of their progeny during pregnancy and before birth, and after parturition human mothers, as in all other mammal species, also routinely control the lives of their dependent progeny for varying amounts of time after birth. Evolutionary selection pressures determined the embodiment of autonomous female mammals. Thus, to understand the evolution of women's autonomy as well as the ongoing selection pressures faced by women in misogynistic human societies, it is useful to be acquainted with the assumptions (the rules) of sexual selection and sexual conflict.

Alfred Russel Wallace and Charles Darwin (1858) described evolution by natural selection, emphasizing what have become known as the assumptions of selection. Natural selection is something that happens because of the phenotypic variants among individuals in a population that are favored or disfavored by environmental or social selection pressures thus "sorting" among individuals so that over time, the traits of "favored" individuals persist and spread (evolve), while the traits of those "disfavored" individuals sometimes disappear entirely – go extinct! Evolutionary fitness is measured as variation among individuals in their lifespan and the lifespan of their children.

Natural selection acting on within-population, within-sex variation in females organized the evolved reproductive traits of female mammals. In human females, evolved reproductive traits include: physiological adaptations associated with age at first menstruation; the subsequent timing and duration of menses; the management of sperm after copulation; timing of implantation of zygotes; the endogenous mechanisms of fetal loss including spontaneous abortion; and the control of developmental milestones during months-long gestation of embryos and fetuses. Selection and adaptation via social-cultural transmission of knowledge further legitimated women in traditional societies to self-administer plant-based contraceptives and abortifacients (Riddle, 1992). Once born, maternal prerogatives include the control of the fate of altricial offspring still dependent on mother's breast milk as well as other milestones of "evolutionary fitness." Just as in other mammals, when variation in women's traits – morphological, physiological, behavioral, and cultural – occur, the opportunity for selection relative to those traits exists. Traits within-populations, within-a-sex that became "fixed" (more or less identical among individuals) indicate that in the past, these traits were "adaptive" – that is, associated with longer maternal life spans and healthier offspring.

Modern institutionalized patriarchy – a social system organized primarily for the benefit of male alliances bent on control of women's sexuality and reproduction – confronts the fundamental rights of every woman to control her own body. Patriarchies can and do produce violent selection pressures that decrease the health, welfare, and lifespan not only of women and their children, but also of men. To understand the origins of women's evolved autonomy one must therefore understand the evolutionary principles of *within-sex selection* and *sexual conflict*.

Within-sex selection is a type of natural selection that occurs among members of the same sex, in a given population of a species. Three assumptions must be met for any selection hypothesis: The first is about the variation in traits of individuals in the "level of selection"; here, the level of selection is within a given species and within a sex. The second posits mechanisms of selection, which impact individuals of a sex differently because of their traits. The third tenet is about "fitness" (length of lifespan and reproductive success of a given individual) that results from the traits because of the mechanisms of selection. Said another way: The three assumptions of within-sex selection are that individuals within a sex, say females, vary in traits that are affected by environmental and social constraints and opportunities, such that some females – because of their traits – live longer or have more or healthier offspring than other mothers. The "competitive" dynamics of within-sex selection among females in all mammal species has guaranteed that mammal mothers who remained in control of their own reproduction were more evolutionarily successful than those mammal mothers without control of their own reproduction. Within-sex selection is a process that results in greater or lesser fitness outcomes for some individuals compared to other individuals *of the same sex because of their traits*, and in the current context, our concern is about within-sex variants associated with any interference with an individual's reproductive decisions.

Sexual conflict is selection that occurs when the reproductive interests of individual females and males disagree. In current misogynistic societies, the focus is on the wins and losses of one sex compared to the other sex; accordingly, in discussions of "the battles of the sexes," it appears that the contestants are a given woman and a man, a given female and a given male (e.g., a woman who was raped and the man who raped her). However, in an evolutionary context, the selection dynamics are between individuals within a sex, among males on the one hand who do and do not rape and, on the other hand, among females who are able to avoid being raped and those who are unable to avoid being raped. Aggressive and coercive sexual conflict is not just about the outcomes – for example, of an aggrieved woman or a violently neutered man (the way we look at rapacious men and angry "castrating women" in the context of crime and litigation). It is about a male and the other males in the population of males and, simultaneously, about a female and the other females in the population of females.

The 19th century evolutionary logic of Darwin and Wallace, then, still holds: Whenever available variation exists among females, the opportunity under sexual conflict for the evolution of female resistance exists. Female resistance might always start with one resistive female, but as the recent #*MeToo* movement demonstrated, resistance can catch on and spread, and thus demonstrating that "sisterhood is powerful." Similarly, evolutionary logic teaches that whenever available variation exists among males, the opportunity under sexual conflict for the evolution of coercive, deadly males exists. What remains interesting from an evolutionary perspective is that not all females are resistive and not all males are coercive. In fact, despite the almost universal control that most mammal females have of their own reproduction, it is remarkable that a hallmark of modern human societies is parental collaborations, which bring up questions about the origins of monogamy. And, thus, we might ask what the fitness outcomes were – among females and among males – in the evolutionary transitions to so-called monogamous marriage. Rape and male coercion of females may have been a defining selection pressure biasing social organizations in many (most) modern societies. How did all that happen?

Millions of years of selection among females in mammal populations has produced the complete, utter (nonautonomous) dependence of young on their mother's ability and willingness to gestate. *This means that, from a natural selection perspective, abortion is solely the prerogative of an individual woman.* It is her choice and her choice alone to end a pregnancy. In addition *it is the inviolable prerogative of a woman to resist the social/political forces that restrict her options; her right is to use her body as she pleases.* Autonomy is embodied in each human individual; autonomy of women is embodied in the hundreds of million years of the evolution of female mammals. And it appears that among the 10,000 mammal species in the world, conspecifics appropriating the bodies of females is rare, perhaps a novelty among mammals. Diminishing female autonomy through religious edict and civil law is a patriarchal imperative, and, it is an abomination against nature that likely will continually reduce the lifespan of women and their offspring.

The evolution of women's resistance to others' control is a relatively obscure topic in evolutionary biology. Women's resistance to other's control – whether conscious or not – is a counter-selection pressure against the patriarchal domination of societies. And, that puts questions about the evolutionary origins of patriarchy under a light: What ancient selection pressures favored male control of female reproduction and women's resistance?

Speculations Abound

For example, could the differences between females and males in dispersal patterns have set up patriarchal advantage? In some primates, including humans, dispersal patterns of daughters and sons differ with sons tending to be more philopatric than their dispersing sisters. Philopatric sons live with or near parents throughout life so that male relatives readily formed coalitions. In contrast dispersing daughters set off as explorers, perhaps seeking strange males for "one night stands" or coalescing with other females to form new groups, aiding discovery of new resources, not to mention longterm bonding with novel males, which is a breeding tactic enhancing the health of offspring producing reproductive success benefits for mothers and fathers. The higher primate tendencies of stay-at-home sons and adventuresome, wandering daughters might mean that it was women who began the dispersals of humans around the globe, away from parental confines. These dispersal patterns meant that males more likely "owned the land" and were buttressed in their power by confederacies of male relatives.

Women's evolved autonomy powers resistance to patriarchy and male control of women's reproductive decisions. Patriarchal control handcuffs the development of societies, guaranteeing brutality that shortens lifespans for women, children, and men.

In October 2019 US District Court Judge Myron Thomson blocked Alabama's near-total abortion ban saying:

> Alabama's abortion ban contravenes clear Supreme Court Case precedent. It violates the right of an individual to privacy,

to make choices central to personal dignity and autonomy. It diminishes the capacity of women to act in society, and to make reproductive decisions. It defies the United States Constitution.

The Judge's ruling is consistent with evolutionary principles.

For Sources and Further Reading

Darwin, C., & Wallace, A. R. (1858). On the tendency of species to form varieties; and on the perpetuation of varieties and species by natural means of selection. *Journal of the Proceedings of the Linnean Society of London. Zoology, 3*, 45–62.

Gowaty, P. A. (1992). Evolutionary biology and feminism. *Human Nature, 3*, 217–249.

Gowaty, P. A. (Ed.). (1997). *Feminism and evolutionary biology: Boundaries, intersections, and frontiers.* New York: Chapman Hall.

Hrdy, S. B. (2000). *Mother Nature: Maternal instincts and how they shape the human species.* New York: Ballantine Books.

Hudson, V. M., Bowen, D. L., & Nielsen P. L. (2019). *The first political order: How sex shapes governance and national security worldwide.* New York: Columbia University Press.

Lerner, G. (1986). *The creation of patriarchy.* New York: Oxford University Press.

Riddle, J. M. (1992). *Contraception and abortion from the ancient world to the Renaissance.* Cambridge, MA: Harvard University Press.

16 Embodiment and the Lived Experience of Diaspora

Bibi Bakare-Yusuf

Becoming displaced from an originary time and space is characteristic of being human. This essay argues that the diasporic experience is at once deeply embodied, universal, and continually constructed through social relations and discursive practices. Fundamental black diasporic moods are thematized in a way that incorporates both pre-discursive and discursive elements.

Diaspora and *embodiment* are terms that have separately gained currency in contemporary critical thought. However, the relations *between* them are inadequately theorized. This is the task ahead. Diaspora should not be taken to be an abstraction concerning the spacing of the subject across time. This movement away from and to a place can only be understood via a third mediating term: "the body" or "embodiment." Place and body support and belong to each other. Being uprooted and rerouted to another place forces dispositioning and repositioning. Embodied orientations are disoriented, and bodies of culture have to be reoriented in each new location. This imperative to rework a cultural patterning in pluralizing new contexts always involves a relationship between traces of "old" practices and engagement with the new situation. Theorization of black diasporic identity and expressive agency, therefore, needs to be grounded in affective social practices, experiences, relations of power, and habits of bodily being.

(In)habiting the Body

Moving away from the Cartesian disembodied consciousness of "I think therefore," Maurice Merleau-Ponty stresses the active embodied "I can." *Incarnated intentionality* refers to the body's capacities to act in the world prior to conscious or reflective thinking according to situational demands. For Merleau-Ponty, my bodily capacities are acquired through habits formed through repeated practice. These capacities are limited by physiological constraints, previous attitudes, and socioeconomic, cultural and historical position. These condition the way I comport myself and inhabit the world.

As embodied subjects, our actions are constituted, limited, and empowered by an interaction between our habitat, history, and biological inheritances. It is within this "already constituted" space that we take up our place in the world, interact with others, and either feel at home or made not to feel at home. The intentional body is always constituted spatially and temporally, and whenever the body takes up the terms of the world, it necessarily transforms the world in the process. So it is that repeated acts of corporeal practice enable a culture to continue and to reinvent itself.

E-motion, Origin, and Freedom

Embodied agents are always grounded in their lived experience. They "inhabit" their body in specific ways: inscribed and circumscribed, social and self-generated. The body referred to here is not merely the physical body conceptualized as a biological object. The body is neither the subject nor the object of experience. It is prior to both. It lies between and yet prior to inner and outer worlds. Through the temporal flow of lived experience, the body as self and the body as world folds and unfolds.

This expressive, situated body continuously reveals the self anew in relation to other bodies and to new situations and roles. The body in motion and the knowledge it bears is shifting and indeterminate. Merleau-Ponty's phenomenology of embodiment can therefore be seen as the prelude to a situated theory of emotions: All motion is the horizon of *e-motion*. Being located or dislocated in space has affective force. Conversely, emotional experience requires a background of some prior sense of orientation (or disorientation) in the world. Displacement from the locus of significance (the "home place") can lead to a shift in mood because bodies no longer feel connected to the familiar geography which grounded their identity and gave them meaning.

Emotion is therefore another name for a specific form of being-in-the-world and "being-to-the-world." Emotions cannot be reduced to pure interiority or a function of the individual psyche; our emotions reveal the dynamic of relations between self/other and world.

Different emotional responses to situations are the expression of changing relations to a changed world-situation. Emotions are not the "objects" of our experience; they are the forms our existence takes. Diasporicity, then, is not simply an experience of motion or displacement, but an experience that induces profound emotional responses: danger and fear, loss and grief, joy and pain.

Conceptualizing embodied diasporic experience within the terms of the sociality of emotions points to a new way of understanding mixed emotional responses to displacement. For example, the tension between the so-called essentialist accounts of the black diaspora and the anti-essentialists, and anti-anti-essentialists, can be resolved by a return to an embodied account of the relationship between emotion and motion. With the expressive, e-motional body, we can begin to understand the relationship between conditions of embodiment and freedom. Understood as a fundamental synthesizing agency, the body becomes a gathering of the past in the present that enables the emergence of new futures. But this is only the active side of a two-sided story. The body's capacity to bring the world into being is based on its passive relation to a preexisting world. If this sounds paradoxical, the contradiction disappears when the relation between the body and the world is understood as a nonoppositional one of mutual interdependency. Embodiment allows a world that is already there to come into being, again. The body renews the world through an "eternal return" and takes up the possibilities offered by the world and repeats and transforms them.

This Merleau-Pontyian horizon of the body's relation to the world has far-reaching implications for thinking origin, displacement, and subjectivity. The world we are located in is imbued with values, traces, and forms of significance that precede our occupation. The world, therefore, has its own intentionality that is prior to our subjective intentions or free will. Yet, the world only has significance when its sedimented values are taken up afresh through practice by each embodied community or subject. For instance, although the *de jure* laws upholding white supremacy in the United States may have been legally abolished, they *de facto* preserve inherited access to economic and cultural privilege and myth-making which White people as a collective continue to benefit from and unwittingly perpetuate. Correspondingly, Black existence remains conditioned by the norms, values, and laws of antebellum society, expressed devastatingly and brutally in structural and existential racism, grinding poverty, and restricted access to economic and cultural means of production.

If freedom is the capacity to act and realize my intentionality, the collective implicated in the "I" has the choice and power to either persist with an oppressive practice or contribute to its demolition. Freedom to perpetuate or reject oppressive practices is, however, grounded in collective sociohistorical processes, privilege, and nonprivilege which form the basis of the exercise of choice. It is as intentional, situated, and inter-corporeal beings that we have a world and are free to act. Through this "worlding" of embodied communication, we take up stylistic gestures, features, resistance, and habits that are specific to our cultural, geographical, economical, and historical situation. This communication is renewed through each encounter and event. Here then, Merleau-Ponty offers a radically different way of thinking about origin and freedom. Paradoxically, origin is always repeating itself and structured through difference. Thanks to the primordiality accorded to difference, as embodied subjects we give birth to the world and new possibilities are generated.

The Ontology of Diaspora

Here, I want to highlight two implications of Merleau-Ponty's corporeal and sensuous phenomenology for a fresh investigation into the terms of diasporic experience. First, his work can be used to show that the experience of diasporicity is deeply embodied and universal. The body is a place, a repository for a certain view of the world, for ways of moving and interacting with others. In turn, a place is a form of the body, a unifying site of historical and cultural forces. Merleau-Ponty calls the intertwining of body and place the "flesh of the world." The implication is that when this flesh of the world becomes disconnected, the corporeal agent can experience acutely the pain of being elsewhere, feeling atopic to their new location in a way that resists cognition or language.

Painful or pleasurable, if the grounding of diasporic experience in the emotionally situated body remains unthought, the historically constituted diasporic subject is problematically conflated with the globe-trotting, multi-passported world traveler. These entrepreneurial and intellectual jet setters are able to celebrate the commodity fetishism of their global access and success, to enjoy the intrigue of diasporicity that is available for appropriation and cultural chic. Historically constituted diasporic communities may uncritically cling to the allure of the original home. Unlike the appropriative elites, those whose journey on the road or sea was forced have experienced violent negation of the freedom of the Merleau-Pontyian corporeal schema. The celebration of the hybrid and the "international beige" is rife with conflict and ineffable agony. These conflicts involve positionings, crises of identity, alienation, and the feeling of being always out of time and off key. Diasporic subjects are forced to reconcile themselves to the fact that their place in the world is what Audre Lorde refers to in her 1984 book, *Sister Outsider,* as the "house of difference rather than the security of any particular difference" (p. 226). The displaced diasporic body can be, and is often, a site of conflict and despair and not the wonderful consumerized, global mish-mash of difference and transgressive hybridity that is celebrated in contemporary theory and popular culture.

The second implication of Merleau-Ponty's account is that through thinking the deep significance of the body–place relation, he offers a radical way of thinking origin. His model refutes a naïve causality of embodied habitus in which the embodied subject acquires competence from repetition of bodily acts grounded in a static culture. The origin for Merleau-Ponty is a *momentary* event that is renewed and reconstituted in the embodied moment of a performative present. Movement away from an original locus means that the origin will be reconstituted in its new context. Merleau-Ponty's insight, then, is that diasporicity is not the result merely of factual changes in location and culture but rather is the outcome of transformatory dialogs between the embodied being and place. What constitutes home or origin opens itself up to be reworked in the present.

As such, Merleau-Ponty's philosophy creates the possibility of an active agency that takes up the preconstituted diasporic complex through the work of the present. Accordingly, paradigms of lament and pain are not a necessary condition of diasporicity. Because origin is a differential repetition, the negative emotionality associated with displacement is open to the play of differences. On these terms, we can talk about the humor, the creativity, and the joy of diasporicity.

The Limit of Merleau-Ponty's Phenomenology

Although Merleau-Ponty theory allows us to think about an embodied diaspora that is at the heart of what it means to be human, there is a serious problem with it. We can only embrace a generalized and metaphysically positioned diaspora if we disregard the question of how we are positioned by and take a position in relation to others. Merleau-Ponty's theory comes up against its limits when we ask the question: "Can you be a diasporic subject and not know it?" The French philosopher would have to answer in the affirmative: It is possible to be unmindful of one's diasporicity due to the unconscious dialog about how one's origins are being reworked. Yet the question proves complicated when we recognize the power of categories such as race, ethnicity, gender, and so on in the formation of identity. The power of being positioned permits us to understand that the construction of subjectivity is not solely the work of the embodied subject.

By stressing the powerful medium of the incarnated agent, Merleau-Ponty fails to explicitly acknowledge the other's work of objectification in social relations. Any account of subjectivity must allow for a moment when the self is constructed through the externalizing power of the other, a moment in which one can only experience the self through the gaze of the other. The body is no longer both subject and object; it becomes objectified or named for others. Any full account of subjectivity must negotiate between auto-constructions of subjectivity and those imposed from the outside, rather than setting them up as opposed. While how I appear to others might condition my habits of being in the world, my whole corporeal trajectory need not be determined by these external limitations or the limitations wrought by my body. Through my power of choice, agency, and action I can (re)create myself through the sociality of my emotions and sociohistorical situatedness.

Diasporicity can be conceptualized, then, as an ontological event, as an achievement, or as an imposition. Some are born diasporic, some achieve diasporicity, and some have it thrust upon them. A crucial limit of Merleau-Ponty's work is that it can only account for the first possibility. By refusing to analyze the differences at work in the social field, Merleau-Ponty's philosophy risks concealing the power relations that constitute it, setting his work adrift as an abstract pre-discursive ontology rather than a concrete social ontology.

Frantz Fanon's seminal essay, "The Lived Experience of the Black," helps us address this shortcoming by providing a discursive and sociohistorical transformativity. On his account, embodied transformativity cannot simply be pre-discursive. Freedom and "dis-alienation" from the prison of appearance involves a reflective account of how "the other" positions the diasporic subject and attempts to naturalize this positioning through an over-investment in the visual register. This discursive and visualized contestation is the framework within which diasporic Black agents negotiate their search for freedom and different modes of being beyond white supremacist logic.

Conclusion

With both Merleau-Ponty and Fanon in mind, we can see how it is possible to bridge the gap between different existential modes and moods of diasporicity, namely the preconscious and the discursive. Cleavage between these two moments is untenable if we acknowledge that through embodiment, both moments are *necessary* for comprehending why diasporicity can be a source of both affirmative celebration of where you are and of melancholia and nostalgia for an originary home. When we begin to understand the evolution of the black diaspora as an ontological condition, the full force of transportation, enslavement, colonialism, and indifference to black humanity comes into sharp relief. On a discursive level, bodies are encoded into a world and ways of being that organize them. For the diasporic black body, this organization bears a distanced and deferred relation to an origin. Despite this distance and hiatus, many diasporic subjects often yearn for an originary past which will anchor their identity, providing emotional stability in a world which disrupts and challenges their existence prior to any form of agency or expression.

For Sources and Further Reading

Bakare-Yusuf, B. (2008) Rethinking diasporicity: Embodiment, emotion, and the displaced origin. *African and Black Diaspora: An International Journal, 1*, 147–158. The present essay is a condensed, revised version of this earlier work.

Part V

Healing

To what new pathways to wholeness and wellness does a view of humans as *fully embodied* point? What insights on individual and collective healing arise from reimagining humans in terms of their energy-emitting and absorbing, mobile, sensate, skin-covered, socially embedded body? The essays in this section take up these questions, with attention to cutting edge perspectives on bioenergy, touch, movement, and technology-assisted embodiment.

17 Vital Energy, Health, and Medicine

Shin Lin and Gaetan Chevalier

The term "Vital Energy" stems from ancient concepts that cannot be defined scientifically. However, the human body produces and responds to a wide spectrum of measurable energies that form the basis of an increasingly large host of medical devices for diagnosis and treatment of many different diseases and disorders.

The Concept of "Vital Energy"

In many ancient cultures, the living human body is thought to have a characteristic energy that is important for good health and provides natural healing strength for fighting diseases and recovering from injuries and disorders. This energy has different names in different countries.

Qi is the Chinese term for this type of energy, commonly used in the context of medicine and martial arts. *Ki* in Japan and Korea, and *prana* in India carry a similar meaning. In Traditional Chinese medicine, *qi* is thought to circulate through channels known as meridians. A strong, balanced flow of *qi* is deemed necessary for good health and healing, whereas deficiency and blockage of *qi* flow results in dysfunction and disease. Inscribed on artifacts thousands of years old unearthed in China, *qi* is not definable in modern scientific terms. Instead, *qi* refers to personal sensations and feelings; they can be sensed, but there are no specific biological markers measurable with scientific instrumentation.

"Vital Energy," "Life Force," and "Biofield" are current Western terms with meaning related to *qi*, *ki*, and *prana*. These forms of energy can be divided into *veritable* (or tangible) and *putative* (or intangible) energy. Veritable energy can be measured with scientific instrumentation, with characteristic frequencies ranging from low-frequency vibrations (e.g., low pitched sound) to higher frequencies in the electromagnetic spectrum (e.g., electricity, visible light); these are sometimes called *bioenergy*. Putative energy is defined as energy that is not measurable with modern scientific instruments. It includes electromagnetic energy so low in magnitude that it cannot be detected with instruments available today and energy that cannot be defined by current scientific paradigms.

Emission and Reception of Energy by the Human Body

A scientific discussion of vital energy begins with the well-established fact that the human body produces and emits many measurable forms of energy. At the most basic level is the emission of thermal energy as infrared rays (frequencies just below visible light); it is easily detectable by touch and quantifiable with household thermometers and infrared cameras. The heart, brain, and muscles produce electrical energy which can be measured by electrocardiography (ECG, or EKG), electroencephalography (EEG), and electromyography (EMG), respectively. The body also emits a low level of magnetic energy, which is detectable with a superconducting quantum interference device (SQUID). The medical technology of magnetoencephalography (MEG) for brain imaging is based on this type of phenomenon. Less well known is the body's emission of light. These emissions, termed *biophotons*, are very low in magnitude but can be measured with highly sensitive devices.

The human body also has many structures that respond to external electromagnetic energy. The most sensitive are the rods in the eye, which respond to individual photons. As elaborated below, other cells and tissues also respond to externally applied electrical energy, which can be shown to affect cells grown in culture.

Changes in Body Energy in Relation to Health and Healing

Elevated body temperature, fever, accompanies many disorders. This phenomenon is measured with a simple thermometer or devices that detect heat in the form of infrared rays. The latter are useful in research and clinical applications (e.g., detection of circulatory abnormalities and inflammation) and in public health settings (e.g., airport screening for travelers with flu-like symptoms).

ECG is routinely used to detect abnormalities in the structure and function of the heart. Heart rate variability (HRV) is increasingly used to evaluate the balance between the sympathetic (fight-or-flight response) and parasympathetic (relaxation response) branches of the autonomic nervous system. Recording EEG to measure changes in brain wave patterns is used in clinical and research settings to study neurological and psychological states.

Research on the relationship between electric fields and wound healing has revealed how this type of energy can alter cellular structure and function. The skin of humans and other animals emits a very low DC electric field under normal conditions, but its intensity increases dramatically during wound healing. In a pioneering study by M. Zhao and collaborators at the University of Aberdeen and other institutions, an externally applied electric field enhanced cell migration in the closing up of artificially created wounds in cell cultures. This effect involved enzymes crucial in cellular signaling pathways, including those that regulate blood vessel development (*angiogenesis*) and cell movement towards chemical attractants (*chemotaxis*). A follow-up study by our research group and collaborators at Hong Kong City University showed that the electrically induced change in cell movement involves rearrangement of the actin cytoskeleton, which is vital for cellular movement and contractility in every type of cell in the body.

Eastern *Qi*-Related Practices and Therapies

Because a state of strong and balanced *qi* is traditionally regarded in Chinese culture as vital to good health and healing, a variety of Eastern therapies and practices are aimed at promoting this desirable state.

Qigong ("exercise for *qi*" in Chinese) is a diverse family of Chinese practices that were historically developed to improve the strength and flow of *qi*. These practices are characterized by the integrated regulation of mind, body, and breath. The best-known practice is *tai chi*, which originated as a martial arts system at the Chen Family Village in Central China about 400 years ago (Chen style *tai chi*). To the practitioner, an indication of enhanced *qi* flow is the tingling, bloated, and warm feeling in the hands. In our laboratory, we used laser Doppler flowmetry to confirm that these sensations correlated with increased blood flow to the hands. Increased blood flow was accompanied by increased flow of electricity, measured deep in the tissue at acupuncture points. The correlation of electrical flow with blood flow is interesting in light of the principle of "blood is the mother of *qi*" described 2,500 years ago in the book *Huangdi Neijing* (Yellow Emperor's Medical Classic). Whereas increased blood circulation is well understood to promote health and healing through elevated transport of oxygen, nutrients, and waste products, increased internal electrical flow and electric field may also enhance healing, as described below.

It is also important to note that randomized controlled clinical trials have shown definitively that *tai chi* can improve many clinically relevant measures of health, including reduction of stress and relief of symptoms of arthritis and fibromyalgia, and enhancement of proprioception, cardiovascular functions, and immune response. A recent functional brain imaging study by J. Tao and collaborators from Fujian University of Traditional Chinese Medicine and other institutions found that *tai chi* and *qigong* practitioners have higher connectivity between the hippocampus and the prefrontal cortex, resulting in enhanced memory and executive function. Studies such as these led *Harvard Health* (August 2019) to call *tai chi* "medication in motion."

In traditional Chinese medicine, the stated intent of many therapies is to "quicken the blood and move the *qi*." Our laboratory has confirmed that therapies such as acupuncture and *dit da jow* (topical herbal medicine used for sprains and bruises) can indeed increase local blood flow. These therapies also produce other beneficial effects on physiological functions, such as inducing production of endorphins for pain relief and regulation of cardiac function.

The most common *qi*-related medical therapy is acupuncture, which involves the addition of physical energy to the body through manually twirling a needle after insertion into an acupuncture point. This needling action distorts underlying connective tissue; cells attached to this tissue are indirectly deformed, leading to the secretion of signaling molecules (e.g., ATP, histamine) that could produce analgesic, anti-inflammatory, and other downstream effects. For some acupuncture points that overlay major nerves, the physical force from the needle can also send signals through the nerves to the brain, resulting in systemic effects throughout the body. J. C. Longhurst's group at our University has found that electroacupuncture, in which electrical pulses are applied through the needles, lowers blood pressure longer than does manual needle manipulation.

A common type of consumer device for relieving muscular pain involves transcutaneous electrical nerve stimulation (TENS; see also the next section). In one version, called transcutaneous acupoint electrical stimulation (TAES), electrodes are placed on acupuncture points. M. Leung's group at Hong Kong Polytechnic University showed that TAES can lower blood sugar in diabetic patients as much as does physical exercise. They also found that aiming a laser at acupuncture points (laser acupuncture) around the knee – similar to the low-level laser treatment used by physical therapists for general pain relief – relieves pain and inflammation and improves mobility in patients with osteoarthritis.

Finally, there is a group of therapies delivered by so-called "energy healers" that includes External *Qi* Therapy from China, *Reiki* and *Johrei* from Japan, *Pranic Healing* from the Philippines, and *Therapeutic Touch, Healing Touch*, and *Polarity Therapy* from the US. An underlying belief is that *qi* or vital energy can be transferred without touching from the hands of a healer to a patient over a range of inches to miles (distance healing). Although there are claims that these therapies derive from ancient practices, they all originated in the 20th century. The few randomized controlled trials on some of these therapies failed to demonstrate unequivocally benefits relative to no-treatment controls. Studies of whether *qi* or vital energy from energy healers affects cells grown in culture either showed no effect or were methodologically deficient. Moreover, there is no scientific explanation of how energy from an "energy healer" could have enough power to influence a patient's physiology without touching, particularly from miles away. Any positive effects of such therapies likely involve the psycho-physiological mechanisms of the placebo effect. The body's responses to a placebo can activate a person's capacity to heal from a variety of pathological conditions.

Western Energy Medical Devices and Therapies

Today, a host of Western medical devices and therapies are based on applying different forms of energy to the human body to enhance health and healing. The most basic devices are lamps emitting energy in the visible spectrum, supplementing sunlight exposure to treat seasonal affective disorder, vitamin D deficiency, and skin disorders. Infrared lamps and chambers warm the body to improve blood circulation and optimize conditions for metabolic processes and other physiological reactions. Newer devices emit far infrared rays, which early-stage research indicates can relieve pain and inflammation without heating the body.

Next are devices emitting electromagnetic fields (EMF). As described above, electric fields have many effects on cellular structures and functions. Common EMF therapies use pulsed electromagnetic field (PEMF) devices, which usually transmit waveforms via antennae near the target tissue. PEMF treatment of pain and some bone fractures have been cleared by the US Food and Drug Administration (FDA), and research on treating osteoarthritis shows promise.

Transcranial magnetic stimulation (TMS) uses a rapidly varying magnetic field to produce electric fields strong enough to alter neuronal activity. The FDA has cleared TMS for treatment-resistant depression, and reports indicate that it may treat other conditions such as bipolar disorders, drug craving, and schizophrenia.

An emerging domain in medicine is electrical stimulation. Several techniques are practiced clinically and are being investigated for new applications, in particular for conditions unresponsive to drug therapies. Vagus nerve stimulation, for example, is FDA-approved for treatment of depression and epilepsy, and deep brain stimulation has been FDA-cleared for treatment of dystonia, tremor, obsessive-compulsive disorder, and Parkinson's disease. These techniques are further being studied to treat other conditions such as anxiety and Tourette syndrome. They are cutting-edge examples of applications of energy-emitting devices for medical diagnostic and therapy.

The marketing of energy devices has sometimes outpaced government regulatory processes. Because of the legalistic difference between the terms "FDA-cleared" and "FDA-approved," consumers should consult healthcare professionals whether a given medical device has been demonstrated to be efficacious in a randomized controlled trial, and avoid using those with claims unsupported by rigorous clinical testing.

Looking Towards the Future

Scientists are making big strides towards understanding the physiological mechanisms underlying acupuncture. A pioneering study by J. S. Han's group at Peking University showed that when electrical pulses of different frequencies are delivered through acupuncture needles, different endorphins are produced by the body for pain relief. Recent studies have revealed that acupuncture can also sensitize opiate receptors, thus reducing the drug dosage needed to achieve the same level of pain relief. This research is vital to improving pain management and overcoming the world-wide opiate addiction crisis.

Another advance comes from clinical research showing that acupressure massage (stimulation by finger pressure instead of needles) is effective for reducing pain, sleep problems, fatigue, and depression. This type of cost-effective self-help remedy is receiving increased attention in the medical and research communities as a way to counter sky-rocketing cost of healthcare in the US.

The use of Western medical devices that deliver various forms of measurable energy is projected to become a $40 billion industry in the next five years. These devices and modernized version of traditional therapies such as electroacupuncture and laser acupuncture activate and elevate our body's natural healing strength. They are shining examples of the current trend of the convergence and integration of modern medical science with the ancient concept of *qi* and other forms of vital energy for optimal treatment of different diseases and disorders.

For Sources and Further Reading

Hintz, K. J., Yount, G. L., Kadar, I., Schwartz, G., Hammerschlag, R., & Lin, S. (2003). Bioenergy definitions and research guidelines. *Alternative Therapies, 9*, A13–A30.

Jahnke, R., Larkey, L., Rogers, C., Etnier, J., & Lin, F. (2010). A comprehensive review of health benefits of *qigong* and *tai chi*. *American Journal of Health Promotion, 24*, 1–25.

Muehsam, D., Chevalier, G., Barsotti, T., & Gurfein, B. T. (2015). An overview of biofield devices. *Global Advances in Health and Medicine, 4*(suppl), 42–51.

Wang, C., Collet, J. P., & Lau, J. (2004). The effect of *tai chi* on health outcomes in patients with chronic conditions: A systematic review. *Archives of Internal Medicine, 164*, 493–501.

18 The Power of Touch

Oxytocin, the "Love Hormone," Is Released by Massage Therapy

Tiffany Field

Oxytocin, the "love hormone," has been increased by massage therapy. A potential mechanism is stimulation of pressure receptors under the skin that calms the nervous system, including reducing the stress hormone cortisol and, in turn, increasing oxytocin. The massage-oxytocin link illustrates the health benefits of direct, active bodily contact.

What we see and hear on digital devices, across a room, or driving down a highway, we experience at a distance. Touch, on the other hand, only happens up close, when our body – our fingertips, lips, chests, toes – comes into direct contact with the world beyond the skin. Touch is intimate, and vital. Skin is our largest and earliest developing sense organ, and research with humans, monkeys, rats, and other species shows that touching and being touched is vital to development and wellbeing from early in life (Field, 2014). Touch deprivation can impair growth and health, and massage therapy helps premature infants thrive, reduces aggression, and improves management of challenges to wellbeing such as cancer, eating disorders, autism, and pain.

The focus here is on research concerning the role of oxytocin in health benefits of massage. Oxytocin is a neuropeptide that is produced in the hypothalamus and has a significant role in the birth, lactation, and social behavior of mammals. It was first labeled the "love hormone" following on research by Sue Carter and her colleagues that showed that mother prairie voles who were more affectionate with their offspring had higher oxytocin levels (see her chapter in Hurlemann & Grinevich, 2018). Their evidence suggested that oxytocin is released in saliva following lactation and massage. Those data were not surprising given that the mother's breasts are being massaged during breastfeeding. And, the infant's mouth is being massaged during breastfeeding. Their findings were corroborated in a 2019 review of 64 studies by Kerr and colleagues, which concluded that massage therapy increased oxytocin levels.

An example of the massage–oxytocin studies is a 2015 study by Tsuji and colleagues in which mothers gave their children 20-minute massages for 20 minutes a day over a three-month period. Saliva samples were taken from the mothers and the children during massage and during a similar non-massage period. During the massage therapy period, both the mothers and their children had higher oxytocin levels compared to their levels during the non-massage period.

In a 2012 study by Morhenn and colleagues (cited in Kerr et al., 2019), 15-minute moderate pressure back massages were given to a group of 65 adults who were compared to a control group. Oxytocin was again increased. Moreover, adrenocorticotropic hormone, nitrous oxide, and beta-endorphin were decreased, which were all positive effects. Shoulder and neck massage also increased oxytocin levels in a 2008 study by Bello and colleagues (cited in Tsuji et al., 2015).

Oxytocin release by massage may be finely tuned to real social stimulation of the skin. In a 2019 study by Li and colleagues on the relationship between massage therapy and oxytocin, 40 adult males were given 10-minute massages either by hand or machine and blood samples were assayed for oxytocin. Oxytocin levels increased after both hand and machine massage, but more significantly after the massages by hand. The participants also assigned more pleasant ratings and reported that they were willing to pay more for massages by hand than by machine. In addition, brain scans suggested that the hand massages activated regions of the brain that are involved in social cognition and reward.

The underlying mechanism for the massage–oxytocin relationship relates to the stimulation of pressure receptors under the skin, as occurs during massage (see Field, 2014, for a review). Comparing the effects of moderate pressure massage and light pressure massage, the nervous system is calmed by the moderate pressure massage and aroused by the light pressure massage. Following moderate pressure massage, heart rate and blood pressure decrease and EEG recordings show greater theta activity suggesting greater relaxation. For example, in a 2012 study by Rapaport and colleagues (cited by Kerr et al., 2019), massage therapy was compared to a touch control condition. Compared to light touch, twice weekly 45-minute Swedish massage sessions significantly decreased cortisol levels and increased oxytocin levels.

The stimulation of pressure receptors under the skin during massage leads to an increase in activity in the vagus nerve, the largest cranial nerve with branches to many parts of the body. Vagal activity, in turn, decreases stress hormones, most especially cortisol. With the decrease in cortisol, there are lawful increases in oxytocin as well as serotonin, the body's natural antidepressant and anti-pain neurotransmitter. Further, with the decrease in cortisol, natural killer cells are saved, leading to enhanced immune function given that natural killer cells kill bacterial, viral, and cancer cells.

These studies highlight the importance of particular forms of touch and the release of oxytocin, the "love hormone," for physical health. Physical health is inextricably tied to cognitive, emotional, and social wellbeing, and so it comes as no surprise that oxytocin is involved not only in the attachment process Sue Carter described in mother voles and their offspring, but also in human social cognition and relationships throughout the lifespan. Oxytocin plays a role in facial recognition, trust, empathy, cooperation, and preference for social groups with which one identifies, in context-sensitive ways (see Hurlemann & Grinevich, 2018). The pervasive effects of oxytocin and its release through touch are rooted in the up-close, body/body contact that has characterized the lives of humans and many other animals over the long sweep of evolutionary time. The adaptive value of touch shaped pressure-sensitive mechanisms in the skin and nervous system and the way they function from early in life, imbuing real-time body contact through massage with its healing power.

For Sources and Further Reading

Field, T. (2014). *Touch*. Cambridge: MIT Press.

Hurlemann, R., & Grinevich, V. (Eds.). (2018). *Behavioral pharmacology of neuropeptides: Oxytocin*. Cham, Switzerland: Springer.

Kerr, F., Wiechula, R., Feo, R., Schultz, T., & Kitson, A. (2019). Neurophysiology of human touch and eye gaze in therapeutic relationships and healing: A scoping view. *JBI Database Systematic Review and Implementation Report*, *17*, 209–247.

Li, Q., Becker, B., Wernicke, J., Chen, Y., Zhang, Y., Li, R., ... Kendrick, K. M. (2019). Foot massage evokes oxytocin release and activation of orbitofrontal cortex and superior temporal sulcus. *Psychoneuroendocrinology*, *101*, 193–203.

Tsuji, S., Yuhi, T., Furuhara, K., Ohta, S., Shimizu, Y., & Higashida, H. (2015). Salivary oxytocin concentrations in seven boys with autism spectrum disorder received massage from their mothers. *Frontiers in Psychiatry*, *6*, 58.

19 Traumatic Embodiment

Traumatic Exposure and Healing

Paula Thomson

Traumatic embodied cognitions disenfranchise individuals from an embodied self that can move freely in the world; they inhabit a self that rapidly resonates with any real or imagined signal of threat. Healing trauma is always a process of healing embodied cognitions, agency, and ownership.

The odds of experiencing a major traumatic event during a lifespan are extremely high, with some estimates as high as 90%. Natural disasters, intentional and non-intentional accidents, the loss of a loved one due to a violent event, life-threatening illnesses, victim of assault (sexual or non-sexual), domestic violence, combat or warzone exposure, terrorist attacks, forced resettlement, political imprisonment, and/or exposure to childhood adversities (abuse, neglect, family dysfunction, violent neighborhoods) all directly engage an embodied self. The body is biologically programmed to respond to events that threaten the integrity of the physical and psychological self. For the majority of people, these events are initially distressing and then recovery processes emerge; however, for some individuals (approximately 10%) recovery remains elusive. They develop posttraumatic stress disorder (PTSD) and suffer the devastating effects of trauma for prolonged periods, and for some, an entire lifetime.

The likelihood of developing PTSD increases when individuals are exposed to prolonged intentional interpersonal trauma or are poly-victimized. This dose effect increases stress symptoms such as anxiety, depression, dissociation, and somatic disorders, as well as PTSD (approximately 12%–40% rate of PTSD in samples with cumulative trauma exposure). With optimal support and emotional resilience some individuals may experience posttraumatic growth, an experience that expands a sense of purpose and meaning. They are able to reduce their stress symptoms as they acquire a sense of wellbeing and hope.

Traumatic Embodiment

According to Bessel van der Kolk (2014), the body keeps the score. The body remembers the traumatic event(s) and reveals these memories through physiologic and behavioral responses, especially when a traumatic memory is triggered. Even preverbal infants encode traumatic events as embodied memories; years later these children continue to reenact early traumatic events in play or behavioral actions. These reenactments have a driven repetitive quality that is highly resistant to change. Affective states such as anxiety or anger may accompany these enactments; however, traumatic enactments may just present as anomalous incongruent actions devoid of emotions. Often traumatic reenactments involve aggressive or sexual behaviors. The impulse to harm the self or others is difficult to inhibit, which makes traumatic reenactments challenging to treat clinically.

In general, embodied cognition implies a memory system that encodes information about physical competencies and contextual perceptual and motor responses to external situations in the physical world. This knowledge is shaped from biological experiences directly gleaned from the human body. When the body or the psyche is rendered helpless and immobilized by a more powerful force during a traumatic event, a loss of physical competency is etched into an embodied cognitive scheme. The perceptual and motor responses during a traumatic event are distorted and differ from the normal array of responses evoked during daily activities. All sensory perceptions are heightened and form "flashes" or "bursts" of images that are burned into long-term memory. The accompanying emotional states of terror and/or rage are deeply entwined into these perceptual images; for some traumatized individuals, emotion is dissociated from the event and they are left in a state of profound depersonalization (alienation from a sense of self) and derealization (the world is perceived as dreamlike).

These emotional or dissociative states are also deeply etched into a cluster of traumatic memories. Physiologic responses evoked during traumatic events are specific, operating as instinctual fixed action patterns of fight, flight, or freeze behaviors. Normal homeostatic states shift into heightened allostatic states that mobilize autonomic and sensory-motor responses necessary for survival. The mind and body are united as a single coherent entity to meet the demands of the traumatic event. When these states persist then physiologic adaptations become maladaptive and influence subsequent behavioral, cognitive, and emotional appraisals. The individual is now neurobiologically reorganized to engage in a world that is filled with constant threat and danger.

Embodied cognition, whether trauma-based or not, operates pre-reflectively; instinctive or intuitive responses are mobilized with incredible precision and accuracy. Individual embodied knowledge enhances understanding about other peoples' movement and intentions as well as informs perceptual understanding about emotional states in others. Interactive multimodal sensory-motor, interoceptive, and emotional processes shape the formation of embodied cognition. It is constructed via the specific body we possess, the physical training we experience, and by the particular context within which embodied cognition is grounded. These conditions operate in every setting throughout the lifespan and are modified by the natural changes and adaptions that result from daily demands and events. Sadly, in extreme traumatic events, the body is often severely injured and physical competencies maybe constrained (i.e., shackled, bound). In every situation, embodied cognition is not merely a causal reaction to cognitive appraisals; rather this system is also integral in forming appraisals. More specifically, traumatic appraisals are always biased towards threat, and even worse, disownership of self and loss of agency. These embodied traumatic memories implicitly influence cognitive appraisals.

Embodied Healing

Traumatic events may directly alter a sense of embodied ownership or a sense of embodied agency. When individuals no longer feel that they have agency over their bodily actions, and even worse, a loss of ownership of their body, a sense of self is disrupted. The traumatic assault destroys a sense of subjectivity; the body becomes an object that is disconnected from embodiment. Extreme levels of dissociation now distort the operation of embodied cognition; numbing, indifference, detachment, and passivity are coupled with perceptual distortions of depersonalization and derealization. Disorientation from the world and the self intensifies feelings of isolation. The goal of somatic practices and expressive therapies is to restore a sense of body ownership, including a sense of agency and the ability to once again engage embodied cognition that is flexible and resilient.

Effective treatment reduces a sense of alienation so body habitus can reemerge.

Activities that promote motor agency and perceptual expansion help ameliorate traumatic embodiment. Change can be achieved through a myriad of somatic approaches that aim to heighten embodied awareness along with enactive engagement. In all trauma treatment, the first phase of treatment is to help establish safety before any traumatic memories and grief are explored. Safety includes skills to regulate arousal and to reengage an adaptive embodied sense of being in the world. During the remembering phase, traumatic embodied memories are slowly disentangled from a general sense of embodied ownership and agency. Individuals can learn to move and "feel" their bodies in motion, and they can disambiguate emotional states of terror and/or rage as they move. States of sadness, joy, pleasure and/or relief emerge as the traumatic memories are dislodged from the body.

Body psychotherapy approaches may include movement-based contemplative practices (Qigong, Tai Chi, Yoga, Feldenkrais Method, Alexander Technique), Somatic Experiencing (processing trapped physiologic arousal responses), sensorimotor approach to psychotherapy (tracking body signals and building body resourcing), somatic therapies (massage, acupuncture, hypnosis, biofeedback, neurofeedback, eye-movement desensitization), dance and movement therapy, expressive arts therapy (integration of art therapy, drama therapy, narrative therapy, embodied expression), and/or exposure therapy. These approaches cultivate a reintegration or enhancement of fundamental embodied cognitive processing such as interoceptive, proprioceptive, and kinesthetic awareness. The approach-avoidance motor system becomes more complex and flexible embodied states emerge as healing from past trauma progresses.

When employing embodied therapeutic modalities, the third phase, recovery, is always incorporated throughout treatment. Reconnection with a resilient sense of self often emerges as body ownership is restored. Body awareness is heightened, and the body becomes a reliable source of memory as well as a source of grounding and reassurance. It is no longer a source of dread; it becomes a home from which embodied cognitions are guideposts while engaging in the world.

Embodied cognition is a complex interplay between self, others, and the world. Body-based trauma therapies draw information from embodied cognition with the goal of facilitating real-time social interactions and contexts that are no longer colored by unresolved traumatic experiences. Effective treatment influences social responses that are rooted in past experiences and memories that are stored and retrieved. Even abstract concepts such as truth, value, and aesthetics can be restored within a dynamic embodied cognitive system. These abstract ideas have their roots in the body; healing from traumatic embodiment provides opportunities to re-engage in these higher abstract concepts that are the bedrock of our humanity.

Conclusion

Embodied cognition is a theory that promotes the concept that the sensory-motor system informs subjective emotional feelings; it is the bedrock for neural constructs of situational-induced feelings. As well, interoception (combination of proprioception and visceroception) directly influences a sense of self, self in relationship to the world, and self that experiences another individual's interoceptive state. Complex neural networks shape these embodied experiences at implicit and explicit levels of awareness. The interplay of these networks operates as embodied cognition. Embodied cognition is powerfully evident in heightened states of joy and awe, as well as the searing effects of traumatic exposure. Traumatic embodied cognitions grip individuals, especially those who struggle with chronic traumatic stress symptoms. They are disenfranchised from an embodied self that can move freely in the world; one that can sense and express an elaborate array of emotional and behavioral responses. Unresolved trauma distorts individuals; they inhabit a body that rapidly resonates with any real or imagined signal of threat. A moral sense of meaning is destroyed as they struggle in a vacillating state of numbness, avoidance, and hyperarousal. Their embodied humanity resides in the "dark night of the soul." Healing trauma is always a process of healing embodied cognitions and embodied agency and ownership.

For Sources and Further Reading

Centers for Disease Control and Prevention. Adverse childhood experiences. https://www.cdc.gov/violenceprevention/acestudy/index.html

Dubi, M., Powell, P., & Gentry, J. E. (2017). *Trauma, PTSD, grief, and loss: The ten competencies for evidence-based treatment.* Eau Claire, WI: PESI Publishing and Media.

Mayo Clinic. Resilience: Build skills to endure hardship. https://www.may-oclinic.org/tests-procedures/resilience-training/in-depth/resilience/art-20046311

Thomson, P., & Jaque, S. V. (2019). *Creativity, trauma, and resilience.* Lanham, MD: Lexington Books.

van der Kolk, B. A. (2014). *The body keeps the score: Brain, mind, and body in the healing of trauma.* New York: Viking.

20 Virtual Embodiment and Embodied Cognition

Effect of Virtual Reality Perspective Taking Tasks on Empathy and Prejudice

Fernanda Herrera

Taking the perspective of others through the use of virtual reality (VR) technology increases empathy and reduces prejudice toward a myriad of social targets. The positive effects of VR perspective taking seem to be attributable to virtual embodiment and embodied cognition.

For most of human history, we perceived our surroundings and functioned based on what our physical bodies were able to sense and do. Later, with the establishment of written language and symbols, we were able to expand our surroundings and learn regardless of whether or not physical bodies were present (e.g., reading a book or listening to a story about a far-off place). Now, with the availability of virtual reality (VR) technology, for the first time in our history we are able to embody different kinds of bodies and explore new virtual environments with our own physical bodies. VR technology can trace its origins to the flight simulators of the 1920s and Ivan Sutherland's head-mounted display (HMD) in the 1960s. However, only recently have technological advances made VR a commercially accessible technology. Since 2015, a plethora of new VR devices have reached the consumer market – Oculus Quest, Google Daydream, VIVE PRO, and the Lenovo Explorer to name a few. These releases increased interest in VR not only as an entertainment technology, but as an education and therapy tool that could also be used to train both emotional responses and physical behaviors.

Most of these VR systems work by replacing the perceptual input of the real world with perceptual input from the virtual environment in real time. This replacement is accomplished by: blocking out visual, auditory, and haptic feedback from the physical world; the continuous tracking of the user's head and body movements; and the immediate rendering of a virtual body and virtual environment in response to the user's movements and behaviors. Thus, some of the unique affordances of VR systems are their ability to immerse users in virtual environments, allow them to embody different kinds of avatars, and elicit feelings of *presence* (i.e., the user's subjective feeling of being inside the virtual environment). One of the main goals of Sutherland's first VR headset was to be able to see anything from any angle. Now, content creators are building VR experiences that allow users to virtually experience the lives of others from the first-person perspective in an effort to increase empathy and reduce prejudice.

The process of taking the perspective of others through the use of VR has been termed Virtual Reality Perspective Taking (VRPT). Traditional perspective taking tasks ask participants to imagine what it would be like to be someone else under certain circumstances and try to understand what that person is feeling. During VRPT tasks, on the other hand, participants actively experience what it is like to be somebody else in an immersive virtual environment through the use of VR technology. VR's ability to elicit strong feelings of presence allows users to viscerally experience what it is like to be someone else and to more deeply understand perspectives other than their own. A growing area of research has leveraged VR's affordances and demonstrated that virtually embodying different perspectives in VR can reduce prejudice and bias, increase understanding and empathy, lead to prosocial behaviors, and increase charitable donations. Furthermore, empirical evidence suggests that VRPT tasks can increase empathy for a myriad of social targets, including the elderly, people with schizophrenia, the homeless, individuals diagnosed with autism and children (see Herrera et al., 2018, for a review).

Despite growing evidence supporting the claim that VRPT tasks can increase empathy and reduce prejudice for specific social targets, a key question remains: *Why* is VR an effective perspective-taking medium? Though research and debate continue, two current approaches to explaining the positive results of VRPT tasks are the *virtual embodiment* of the social target and *embodied cognition*. These two theoretical explanations of the effectiveness of VRPT tasks are synthesized below.

Virtual Embodiment

In computer-generated immersive virtual environments, users are usually represented by *avatars*. An avatar is a digital representation of users that are controlled in real-time. Even though the most common avatars available are human-like, users are able to embody a plethora of different virtual bodies (e.g., aliens, cows, or even pieces of coral). Because virtual environments are digitally created and programmed, when participants choose to embody a human-like avatar, they are able to embody avatars that may or may not look like them; avatars may be taller, skinnier, or have a different skin tone than the user. The type of avatar users embody can impact self-perception, attitudes, and behavior both inside and outside the virtual environment. For example, when participants embodied avatars that were taller during a negotiation task inside a virtual environment, they were less willing to accept unfair offers than their counterparts who embodied shorter avatars. Additionally, the behaviors exhibited inside the virtual environment carried over to the physical world regardless of participant's actual height (Yee & Bailenson, 2007, cited in Seinfeld et al., 2018).

Interestingly, when users embody different types of avatars, they experience the *body ownership illusion*. The body ownership illusion refers to the illusory perception a person has in which they believe an artificial body or body part is their own and is the source of physical sensations. An example of this type of body ownership is the rubber hand illusion. The rubber hand illusion consists of hiding a participant's hand and visually replacing it with a rubber hand while simultaneously stroking both the participant's hidden hand and the rubber hand at the same time. This process has been shown to elicit a strong illusion of ownership over the rubber hand and has been found to extend to virtual bodies inside immersive virtual environments as well. More research in this area provided evidence that the body ownership illusion was not only possible for virtual body parts, but for complete virtual bodies as well.

Eliciting the body ownership illusion inside *immersive virtual environments* (IVE) requires several conditions. Users must wear an HMD (to block out their own physical body) and experience the virtual environment from the first-person perspective. They also must perceive their avatar's body in some way, such as using a virtual mirror or by allowing users to look down and see their avatar's body. Finally, the user's avatar must exhibit *visuomotor-synchrony* (i.e., as users move their physical bodies, they can see that their body controls the body of their avatar in real time). Body ownership illusions can reshape social cognition (see Herrera et al., 2018, for primary sources). They are able to mitigate stereotypes and reduce implicit racial biases when participants embody avatars that look like outgroup members. For example, in 2016 Oh and colleagues showed that negative stereotyping of the elderly was reduced by participants who embodied elderly avatars in comparison to participants who embodied a young avatar. Similarly, in 2013, Peck and colleagues found that when white participants embody dark-skinned avatars and experience the body ownership illusion, implicit racial biases are significantly reduced when compared to participants who embodied light-skinned avatars. In an extension of this work, researchers found that after embodying a dark-skinned avatar for about 12 minutes reduces implicit racial bias in comparison to participants who embodied light-skinned avatars or purple-skinned avatars.

Recently, the body ownership illusion has been found to help domestic violence offenders better recognize facial expressions in women. After embodying the body of a female victim in an IVE depicting domestic violence, offenders improved their ability to recognize fearful female faces and reduced their bias to recognize fearful faces as happy (Seinfeld et al., 2018). These results suggest that virtual embodiment can be leveraged to not only change participant's perception, attitudes, and behavior, but that it can potentially be used as rehabilitation tool.

Embodied Cognition

Embodied cognition theory postulates that cognition is an interaction of the body and mind. In contrast to traditional cognitive theories which suggest that a person's knowledge and representations of the world are based on amodal and abstract content, embodied cognition theory suggests that cognition is *situated*. In other words, cognitive activity takes place within the context of the surrounding environment. When an event occurs, the underlying sensory, somatic, and motor states are stored, and when the event is remembered, the original states are partially simulated. Thus, the interpretation and memory of a particular event is rooted in the interaction of both cognitive and bodily states. While virtual embodiment requires users to embody an avatar and experience the body ownership illusion, the embodied cognition explanation differs markedly in that it does not require users to embody any kind of avatar, but rather suggests that simply being able to move around and interact with the virtual environment in naturalistic ways allows users to better understand and empathize with perspectives other than their own.

Traditional perspective-taking tasks, although effective, rely mostly on imagination (i.e., cognitive states). In contrast, VRPT tasks allow users to viscerally experience other people's circumstances as if they were happening to them by allowing users to physically react to the virtual experience. VRPT tasks thus activate the same sensory, somatic, and motor states that would be activated if the experience was happening to the user in real life. Compared to traditional perspective taking tasks, VRPT tasks allow for the interaction of both cognitive and whole-body states, which could lead to a more accurate interpretation of the virtual experience, and thus, a better understanding of other people's perspectives and circumstances.

Moreover, bodily responses during interactions with novel objects have been found to influence later-reported attitudes and impressions. Physical movement can improve a participant's performance while completing cognitive tasks, and the physical experience of a particular environment can have an effect on both perceptions and behaviors. VR allows users to move and interact with their surroundings as if they were actually there through a combination of physical body movements (e.g., walking, extending their arms to reach an object, or turning their head around to examine their surroundings) and button presses. Because of these affordances, users are able to gather spatial information about the virtual environment using the same perceptual systems they would use to gather spatial information about the real world. Thus, the user's ability to actively engage with and move around inside an immersive virtual environment may result in improved cognition due to the additional information users are able to collect through physical movement and allow users to more effectively understand and share the feelings of those they are taking the perspective of, resulting in increased empathy and prosocial behaviors as well as reduced prejudice. These results provide evidence supporting the integration of cognitive and bodily states during perspective taking tasks and suggest that movement is an integral part of VRPT tasks' success.

Conclusion

Overall, VRPT has been shown to consistently increase empathy, reduce prejudice, and promote prosocial behaviors toward different social targets. Across the VRPT literature, researchers suggest that virtual embodiment or embodied cognition may be the mechanisms through which VRPT increases empathy and reduces prejudice. Despite the lack of consensus on the mechanism that leads to the positive results of VRPT tasks, the explanations put forth by researchers highlight the benefits of being able to experience virtual environments with naturalistic body movements, especially in comparison to mental tasks that rely on imagination alone. Moreover, embodying virtual bodies that look different than our own can have important psychological and social effects on the way we perceive ourselves and others. However, more empirical work is needed to further understand the extent to which virtual embodiment and embodied cognition lead to the positive benefits of VRPT, and examine the interaction between them in order to be able to answer what specifically makes VR an effective perspective-taking medium.

For Sources and Further Reading

Ahn, S. J., Bostick, J., Ogle, E., Nowak, K. L., McGillicuddy, K. T., & Bailenson, J. N. (2016). Experiencing nature: Embodying animals in immersive virtual environments increases inclusion of nature in self and involvement with nature. *Journal of Computer-Mediated Communication*, *21*(6), 399–419.

Herrera, F., Bailenson, J., Weisz, E., Ogle, E., & Zaki, J. (2018). Building long-term empathy: A large-scale comparison of traditional and virtual reality perspective-taking. *PloS One*, *13*(10), e0204494.

Seinfeld, S., Arroyo-Palacios, J., Iruretagoyena, G., Hortensius, R., Zapata, L. E., Borland, D., ... Sanchez-Vives, M. V. (2018). Offenders become the victim in virtual reality: Impact of changing perspective in domestic violence. *Scientific Reports*, *8*(1), 2692.

Won, A. S., Perone, B., Friend, M., & Bailenson, J. N. (2016). Identifying anxiety through tracked head movements in a virtual classroom. *Cyberpsychology, Behavior, and Social Networking*, *19*(6), 380–387.

Epilogue
What Embodiment Is

Anthony Chemero

This essay highlights some ways in which embodiment has been misunderstood – leading to misguided critiques of embodied cognitive science– and corrects those misunderstandings. I will explain what embodiment, at least as it is understood by embodied cognitive scientists, really is. Going forward, inquiry based on a sound, shared understanding of embodiment can continue to transform the scholarly landscape.

I have been arguing for the centrality of embodiment in cognitive science and the philosophy of mind for a long time now. Although there are still persistent, long-term critics of embodiment in these disciplines, its centrality has become more widely accepted over time. As the affiliations of the authors in this essay collection make clear, this is true outside cognitive science and philosophy of mind as well: The authors here are drawn from every corner of the university. Despite the increasing acceptance of embodiment in the cognitive sciences, a few new critiques have shown up, mostly driven by social media, where anyone can opine about anything without worrying about the annoying details (editors, peer review) that make old-fashioned academic discourse so difficult. And so slow. This short essay will be reviewed and edited by people with relevant PhDs and will appear in print more than a year after the process began. Given this, it is easy to see the appeal of vomiting one's opinions out into the ether, instantaneously and with no interference from experts. Don't worry, dear reader: The rest of this essay is not a rant about the corrosive effects of social media, a conversation better had over a beer. But I will be responding here to some views of embodied cognition that have gotten attention on social media, among other venues, despite being based on misunderstandings. Unfortunately, even though academics ought to know better, social media fights really do shape academic discourse. So dispelling mis-understandings matters. In this essay, I will point to two objections to embodied cognition. I will argue that both objections are based on a misconception of what embodied cognition is.

The first objection is that the replication crisis plaguing psychology is hitting embodied cognitive science especially hard. A Twitter up-roar about this topic culminated in a January 2019 article in the online magazine *Quartz* by Olivia Goldhill. The article was titled "The repli-cation crisis is killing psychologists' theory of how the body influences the mind," and was published with the ironic page header "Loss of Power Pose":

> But, in recent years, psychology's replication crisis, where rec-reations of major studies failed to produce the same results as the originals, has shown that several crucial findings in the field of embodied cognition fail to hold up. As a result, there are now cynics within psychology who argue the entire field is suspect – as well as die-hard embodied-cognition researchers who insist their theories are sound. The replication crisis has discredited countless individual findings within psychology (and the sciences more broadly) but, in this case, an entire dis-cipline is under attack. (Paragraph 2)

There is some truth to this breathless declaration. Embodied cog-nition has always been under attack. That is how science works: Ideas and findings are scrutinized from every angle, and many scrutinizers are unsympathetic. In this respect, embodied cogni-tion is no more or less under attack than other disciplines. This is also not what Goldhill was talking about. She was talking about Twitter, where a few Tweeters were predicting the demise of embod-ied cognition because of the replication crisis. These tweets were in response to five failures to replicate notable experiments. The original, unreplicated findings were all published in top journals and discussed in the media. Indeed, one of them – the power pose in the ironic page header (Carney et al., 2010) – landed its principal investigator a TED talk. In this research, Carney and colleagues re-ported that adopting a high-power pose – standing upright, looking forward, feet at shoulder width – for a short time changed hormone levels and increased confidence. Other studies that have failed to replicate include that holding a warm cup makes you judge others' personalities as being warmer (Williams & Bargh, 2008); washing your hands makes you feel less guilty about unethical behavior

(Zhong & Liljenquist, 2006); exposure to stereotypes about the elderly makes you walk more slowly (Bargh et al., 1996). (For citations for these and other examples, see Hughes, 2018.) One such finding – that you understand sentences about metaphorical actions more quickly (or slowly) when they align (or conflict) with the bodily actions you must engage in order to show that you understand them (Glenberg & Kaschak, 2002), termed the *action-sentence compatibility effect* – was called "a hallmark finding in Embodied Cognition" in the publication reporting failures to replicate it (Papesh, 2015). Similar things have been said about the others. If these are indeed hallmark findings of embodied cognition and they are failing to replicate, maybe embodied cognition really is in trouble.

The second misunderstanding has not gotten any press, because as far as I know, no one has bothered to make a publishable argument for it. But it comes up frequently when I give talks, and in anonymous referee comments on papers and grant proposals. People often object to my empirical research because most of our experiments are done in virtual environments. The objection is that the very existence and immersivity of virtual environments shows that actual environments and actual bodies don't matter; all that matters is what is represented in the brain. As research in the cognitive sciences increasingly moves into virtual environments, and as replicability concerns persist, perhaps embodied cognition – which insists that real bodies and real environments matter – is in trouble.

But really, embodied cognition is not in trouble. Both objections depend upon misunderstandings of the nature of embodiment. There are two considerations that are fundamental to embodied cognition: *phenomenology* and *perception–action coupling*. First, we can see embodied cognition's roots in phenomenology, especially that of Maurice Merleau-Ponty. To see the centrality of Merleau-Ponty, it is sufficient to look at the two more recent, historical inspirations for embodied cognition: Gibsonian ecological psychology and enactive cognitive science. Both movements are profoundly indebted to Merleau-Ponty's phenomenological philosophy. Any reader of the literature in enactive cognitive science will see Merleau-Ponty's name all over it. Varela, Thompson, and Rosch's book *The Embodied Mind* (1991), the Old Testament of enactive cognitive science, has literally dozens of mentions of Merleau-Ponty and several detailed passages discussing his ideas. Merleau-Ponty's influence on ecological psychology is harder to see: The Old Testament of ecological psychology, Gibson's book *The Ecological Approach to Visual Perception* (1979) never mentions

Merleau-Ponty. But James Gibson clearly was reading him carefully in the years leading up to the writing of *The Ecological Approach*. For one thing, Gibson taught a seminar on Merleau-Ponty's *The Phenomenology of Perception* (1945/1962) in the early 1970s. For another, Bill Mace has spent some time digging through the Gibson archives at Cornell University and, as he reported at the 2014 meeting of the International Society of Ecological Psychology, he found Gibson's page-by-page notes on *The Phenomenology of Perception*. In several cases those notes stray from Merleau-Ponty's text and develop ideas that are key to *The Ecological Approach*.

The key innovation in Merleau-Ponty's phenomenological philosophy is his development of the concept of the *lived body*, which is based on a distinction made by Husserl. The lived body is not a physical object in the world; instead it is a set of bodily skills, habits, and readinesses to act that make the world appear to us in the way that it does. The lived body opens up the world to us as full of possibilities for action. We do not consciously entertain these possibilities, or think about them, or imagine them. Rather, given our bodily skills, habits, and readiness to act – i.e., our lived bodies – we are open to the possibilities to act that make up the world that we experience. If our lived bodies were different, we would experience the world differently. (And we do! The world is experienced differently by those with different skills, habits, and readinesses to act.) If we did not have skills, habits, and readinesses to act, we would not experience the world at all. These considerations are central in the development of the *enactive* and *ecological* approaches to cognitive science: For ecological psychologists, the theory of affordances (see Chemero, 2009) is a theory of the world as we experience it, in terms of what we can do; for enactive cognitive scientists, "laying down a path in walking" (Varela et al., 1991, p. 237, cited in Chemero, 2009) is a matter of constituting an experienced world with bodily actions.

The second fundamental part of embodied cognitive science – the tight connection between perceiving and acting – is built into Merleau-Ponty's views, but it gets a fuller account in the scientific work concerning embodied cognition. I will recount one example here: work on vision and postural sway (Balasubramaniam et al., 2000). When standing, humans are constantly swaying slightly, traversing a few degrees at the ankles, which amounts to a few inches at typical adult human eye height. This sway is predominantly forward and backward, and side-to-side to a lesser extent. Balasubrmaniam and colleagues asked why this was the case. Their hypothesis was that front-to-back postural sway predominates because it is crucial for visually guided action, and not because of anatomical features of the human body (like the direction the feet point). Moving the eyes (or a camera) forward and backward leads to visual motion parallax; it can be shown that visual motion parallax is lawfully related to the distance of objects that you see. Knowing how the distances of objects change is crucial to maintaining your balance: If the distances of objects you see is decreasing rapidly, you are probably about to have an accident, either because you are falling forward or walking into something. To show that front-to-back postural sway serves this visual function, Balasubramaniam and colleagues did a series of simple experiments. First, they had participants face forward and aim a laser pointer at a small target. As expected, postural sway was predominantly front-to-back. Next they had participants face to the side and point a laser pointer at a target to the side. In this case, postural sway is predominantly side-to-side. That is, in both cases, participants sway predominantly in the direction they are looking, generating motion parallax that enables them to see the distance of objects around them. These findings illustrate the second general point of embodied cognitive science: Perception and action are inseparable from one another. Perception is for action, and action is for perception.

We can see from these two fundamentals of embodied cognitive science that the discipline is not in trouble from the replication crisis. Do any of the failures to replicate above have anything to do with the inseparability of perception and action? They do not. All of those studies took up how features of body affect the way we make judgments. Obviously, things that happen to our bodies affect our minds. This is not what is supposed to be interesting about all of those studies that failed to replicate. What made the studies of interest to high impact journals and science journalists was that they seemed to show that what happens to our bodies affects our minds in improbable ways. The very improbability of these findings made them unlikely to be replicable. Some (hopefully small) percentage of scientific studies uncover regularities that are peculiar to the set of participants they examined, or are caused by some uncontrolled variable, or are just chance. The ones that are newsworthy because they are so surprising are the ones most likely to be spurious. But – and this is the real point – none of the findings that have infamously failed to replicate are central to embodied cognitive science. Newsworthy, yes; hallmarks of the approach, no. In saying this, I am echoing Andrew Wilson and Sabrina Golonka when they argue, correctly, in their 2013 *Frontiers in Psychology* article titled "Embodied cognition is not what you think it is," that warm cups and warm feelings are not just not central to embodied cognitive science, but are not embodied cognitive science at all.

Embodied cognition studies the necessity of the living, skilled, ready-to-act body for the very having of experiences; no readiness-to-act means no experience. Embodied cognition studies the close coupling, even the inseparability, of perception and action. If findings on postural sway, visually guided actions, and coordination dynamics fail to replicate, embodied cognitive science would genuinely be in trouble. Central findings in these would be unlikely to fail to replicate because they have already been replicated over and over; moreover, they are generally not sexy enough to raise the eyebrows of those who attempt to (fail to) replicate sexy findings.

Finally, realizing that the core of embodied cognition is the tight coupling of perception and action makes clear that embodied cognitive science and virtual environments are a natural fit for one another. In virtual reality, we can actually manipulate the coupling between perception and action. By turning up visual gain, we can make anyone feel capable of dunking a basketball. By decoupling the relationship between where something looks to be and where it sounds to be, we can explore the relationship between visual and auditory localization, each of which requires different bodily movements (Sanches et al., 2019). In other words, in virtual environments, we can make features of embodiment into independent variables, manipulable by the experimenter. Far from being inconsistent with one another, virtual environments will be crucial in studying the embodied mind.

Embodiment has already transformed many disciplines across academia. In this essay, I have focused on its place in the cognitive sciences. But because embodiment is an inherently interdisciplinary, the points I make here are not limited to the cognitive sciences. Embodiment can continue to impact the arts, humanities, and sciences, and can continue to start conversations that cross boundaries, especially when we are not misled about what embodiment is.

For Sources and Further Reading

Balasubramaniam, R., Riley, M., & Turvey, M. (2000). Specificity of postural sway to the demands of a precision task. *Gait & Posture, 11*, 12–24.

Chemero, A. (2009). *Radical embodied cognitive science.* Cambridge: MIT Press.

Hughes, B. (2018). *Psychology in crisis.* London: Macmillan Publishers Ltd.

Papesh, M. H. (2015). Just out of reach: On the reliability of the action-sentence compatibility effect. *Journal of Experimental Psychology: General,* 144, e116–e141.

Sanches, G., Riehm, C., & Annand, C. (2019). Bee-ing in the world: Phenomenology, cognitive science, and interactivity in a novel insect-tracking task. In A. K. Goel, C. M. Seifert, & C. Freksa (Eds.), *Proceedings of the 41st Annual Meeting of the Cognitive Science Society* (pp. 1008–1013). Montreal: QB Cognitive Science Society.

Index

Note: *Italic* page numbers refer to figures.

For Product Safety Concerns and Information please contact our EU
representative GPSR@taylorandfrancis.com
Taylor & Francis Verlag GmbH, Kaufingerstraße 24, 80331 München, Germany

www.ingramcontent.com/pod-product-compliance
Lightning Source LLC
Chambersburg PA
CBHW061742270326
41928CB00011B/2348

9 7 8 0 3 6 7 5 6 0 4 7 8